Sacagawea
SPEAKS

Sacagawea SPEAKS

Beyond the Shining Mountains with Lewis & Clark

BY JOYCE BADGLEY HUNSAKER

TWODOT

A TwoDot Book
Copyright © 2001 by Joyce Badgley Hunsaker

Published by The Globe Pequot Press, Guilford, Connecticut
TwoDot is an imprint of The Globe Pequot Press

Project developed and managed by Towanda, Inc., Boise, Idaho
General Project Manager: Kathy Gaudry
Editor: Maggie Chenore
Art Director: Gerald A. Arrington, Arrington Design
Preliminary Production and Typesetting: Gail Ward

Cover Photo: Portrait of Joyce Badgley Hunsaker while performing Sacagawea is superimposed over photograph of the Sawtooth Wilderness in Idaho (Photo by David Whitten)

Library of Congress Cataloging-in-Publication Data

Hunsaker, Joyce Badgley.
    Sacagawea speaks : beyond the shining mountains with Lewis and Clark/Joyce
Badgley Hunsaker.
        p. cm.
    Includes bibliographical references and index.
    ISBN 1-58592-079-7
    1. Sacagawea, 1786-1884. 2. Shoshoni women--Biography. 3. Lewis and Clark
Expedition (1804-1806) 1. Title.

F592.7.S123 S35 2001
978.004'9745'0092--dc21
[B]
                                                                                                00-064857

For extra copies of this book and information about other TwoDot books,
write The Globe Pequot Press, P.O. Box 480, Guilford, CT 06437; or call 1–800–243–0495.

Manufactured in Korea
First Edition/First Printing

For the Old Ones
    with gratitude and respect.

For the women of my clan
    past, present, and future.

For Mother.

Contents

In each generation, there are those who become the Story Keepers. I come from a long line of such chosen ones. Whether encoded in songs, ceremonies, recipes, or flower gardens, the stories bound me together with my ancestors. They made me certain of my own unique place within the eternal Circle.

I never tired of hearing the stories of the Old Ones. Each familiar telling left me stronger, wiser, more attuned to the rhythms of living. I learned that every life toils in heroic struggles; every life cradles universal truths. When we listen with our hearts and spirits, much more is made clear to us than when we rely only on our ears.

It is with the deepest respect, then, that I share this story of the historical person Sacagawea. She was an ordinary woman thrust into extraordinary circumstances. She made history simply by being herself.

So it is with each of us.

May the history we create together be one of honor and truth.

Acknowledgments

It is my honor to thank, once again, the Sacagawea family descendants who have endorsed this book, especially Saundra Todd and Eileen Charbonneau.

To my performance audiences—past, present, and future—thank you for allowing me to give voice to the silent past. Creating "living history" carries with it the rare privilege and profound responsibility to move the heart, and open the imagination with truth. It is a dynamic partnership between teller and listener. Our stories together enrich my life more than you can ever know. May they continue to enrich and illuminate yours.

My sincere appreciation goes to all those who have lent their expertise, their enthusiasm, and their spirit to this book. Thank you to the Story Keepers, historians, archivists, and curators who have graciously and unfailingly accessed, then shared, their treasures. To all at Towanda, Inc. and Falcon Publishing, it has been a pleasure sharing this "journey of rediscovery" with you.

A debt of gratitude goes to the site directors and staffs of the USDI Bureau of Land Management's Pompey's Pillar National Historic Site (Billings, MT), and the National Historic Oregon Trail Interpretive Center (Baker City, OR); the USDI National Park Service's Fort Clatsop National Monument (Astoria, OR); the USDA Forest Service's Lewis and Clark Trail Interpretive Center (Great Falls, MT); and the North Dakota Lewis and Clark Interpretive Center (Washburn, ND) To the Lewis and Clark Trail Heritage Foundation goes my continuing respect and admiration, with special kudos to the late Irving Anderson.

Finally, I would like to acknowledge the circle of my family for keeping stories of the Old Ones alive, not only for me . . . but for the generations yet to come. May this work honor you. May this work honor The People.

Mitakuye oyasin.
We are all related.
JBH

Introduction:
Who was Sacagawea?

Ordinary people make history. Sometimes they find themselves in extraordinary circumstances that call for sacrifice or heroism. Sometimes they discover truths that were previously unknown. Sometimes they make history simply by putting one foot in front of the other, day after day after day, until finally they reach places only dreamed of.

So it was with Sacagawea. Fanciful images of her have appeared on film, paintings, postage stamps, crockery, comic books, and a US coin. More statues have been dedicated to her than to any other woman in the United States. Everyone has heard of the teenaged Shoshone mother who carried her baby across two thousand miles of wilderness–and back–on the Lewis and Clark Expedition. Yet few know who she was, as a person. Scholars cannot even agree on how to spell her name.

Sacagawea was an ordinary tribal woman who led an extraordinary life, not only during her trek with the Corps of Discovery, but from the time when, as a young girl, she was taken from the Shoshone by those Lewis and Clark called "Minnetaree." Tribal accounts of the Bird Woman give us insight into her resourcefulness, her inner strength, how she related to others, and what she thought of her life. Written accounts from the Expedition journals view her through her actions–impressions recorded by men outside her culture who could not even speak the same languages Sacagawea spoke.

To clearly understand what really happened in her life and why, we must listen to the stories of the Elders. We must search the written records of that long-ago time. We must learn the lessons of the land she lived upon, and later crossed.

Sacagawea was not an icon. She had strengths and weaknesses, just as we do. She sometimes made mistakes and had regrets. She endured the unimaginable and surmounted the impossible. Her life left its imprint on history.

Her life leaves its imprint on us today.

Sacagawea Speaks

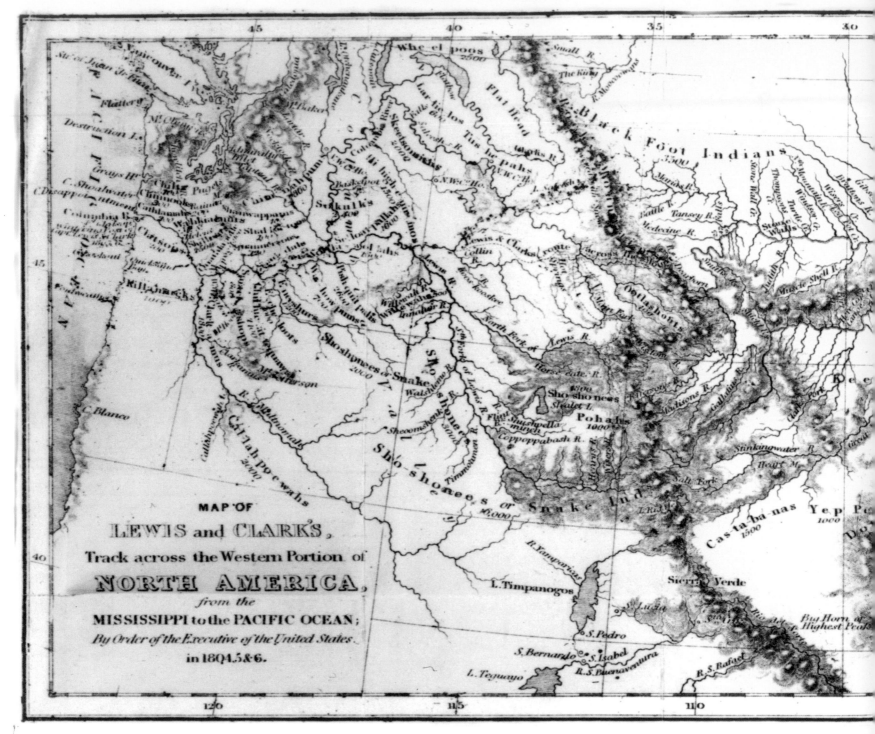

President Jefferson's Instructions to Lewis
Washington, DC
June 20, 1803

"The object of your mission is to explore the Missouri River and such principal stream of it as, by its course and communication with the waters of the Pacific Ocean, may offer the most direct and practicable water communication across the continent, for the purpose of commerce."

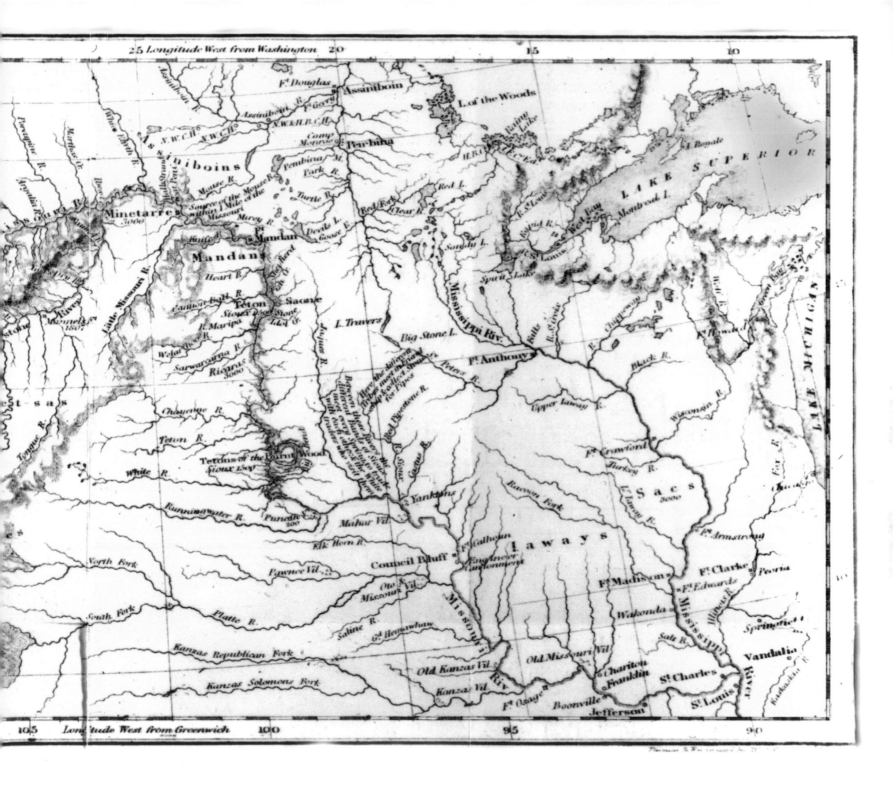

Assiniboin R.
Ft Douglas
Ft Gorry
N.W.&H.B.C.H.
Assiniboin
L. of the Woods
I. Royale
LAKE SUPERIOR
MICHIGAN
Camp Monroe
Pembina
Pembina R.
Park R.
Red L.
Montreal I.
West Bay
Sininiboins
Mouse R.
Turtle R.
Red Fork
Clear R.
Source of the Mouse R. within 1 Mile of the Missouri
Mirey R.
Devils L.
Goose R.
Sandy L.
Minetarres 3000
Mandan
Knife R.
Spirit Lake
Mandans
Heart R.
Fish Cr.
Teton
Sacsie
Stone
R. Maripa
Sioux Wood R.
L. del Q.
Mississippi Riv.
Big Stone L.
L. Travers
Ft Anthony
Peters R.
Black R.
Chayenne R.
Sarwarcarna R.
Ricaras 3000
Jaques R.
Red Pipestone R.
Upper Iaway R.
Wisconsin R.
Teton R.
White R.
Tetons of the Burnt Wood Sioux 1500
Grene R.
Ft Crawford
Turkey R.
Sacs 3000
Runningwater R.
Puncah 200
Mahar Vil.
Yanktons
Racoon Fork
Elk Horn R.
Ft Armstrong
Iaways
Ft Calhoun
Engineer Cantonment
Pawnee Vil.
Council Bluff
North Fork
Ft Clarke
Peoria
Oto & Missouri Vil.
Ft Madison
Ft Edwards
South Fork
Platte R.
Saline R.
Gd Nemawhaw
Missouri
Wakonda
Springfield
Kanzas Republican Fork
Old Missouri Vil.
Mississippi River
Vandalia
Old Kanzas Vil.
Chariton
St Charles
Kanzas Solomons Fork
Kanza Vil.
Salt R.
Franklin
Ft Osage
Boonville
St Louis
Jefferson

Clusters of mountain ash berries splash granite-strewn banks of the Pack River, Selkirk Mountains, Idaho.

Sacagawea Speaks...

Some say my name is Sah-KAH-gah-WEE-ah. Some say SACK-ah-ja-WEE-ah. Still others, Tsa-KAH-kah-WEE-ah, or Sah-KAH-joo-ah. My own husband rarely called me the same name twice, usually settling for "Squaw,"[1] "Woman," or just "You." Chiefs Lewis and Clark did the same, but they added "Janey" because it was easy for their tongues to say. And when they named a river for me, they called it Bird Woman's River.[2]

When my son was born, among my clan I became a new name: "Mother of Pomp."[3] That is how I have thought of myself ever since.

I was born among the Numa Agui Dika,[4] the "Salmon Eaters," sometimes called the "Snakes" from the Shoshoni hand sign that was misunderstood by the white men. To us, the sign looked like the tail of the salmon as it swam upstream. To the whites, the same sign looked like the motion of a snake.[5] So they called us Snake, or Shoshone.

There were many small bands of us in those days—each having clans—scattered across the land. I learned the ways of my people as all young girls do, under the watchful eyes of the elders. All the women of my clan I called "mother," "sister," "grandmother." All the men, I called "father," "brother," "grandfather." This is how we were known to each other in the old days.

Clark   March 11, 1805

"We have every reason to believe that our Minnetaree interpreter [Charbonneau] (whom we intended to take—with his wife—as an interpreter through his wife to the Snake Indians, of which nation she is) has been corrupted. . . . We give him tonight to reflect and determine whether or not he intends to go with us under the regulations stated."

Numa Agui Dika
  (nuh-MAH ah-GUY dee-kah)
  (neh-MAH ah-GUY dee-kah)
Shoshone *(show-SHOWN)*
Shoshoni *(show-SHOWN-ee)*

Camas Roots and Bulbs, Root-Gathering Implement

The basket (upper right) is woven of plant fibers and exhibits a geometric design. It is filled with Common Camas, the most important food root harvested by the Nez Perce. Common Camas (*Camassia quamash*) grows over a vast geographical range: from British Columbia to California, and east to southwest Alberta, Montana, Wyoming, and Utah. Vigilant throughout the camas's seasonal cycle, the Nez Perce waited as the blue flowers withered and fell off in late spring to early summer, then dug the roots from July through September. Bulbs were steamed in pit ovens, then dried and ground into flour. There is a poisonous form of camas called Death Camas. To avoid confusion at harvest time, the native peoples bent the stems of the Common Camas in spring, when the telltale blue blossoms were visible.

This bone-handled root-digging stick is precisely the type seen by Lewis and Clark. Its shaft is made of straight-grained wood; the digging point has been slow-charred, then repeatedly oiled to make it extremely hard.

Camas flowers blanket the Little Camas Prairie, Idaho.

Every year we traveled beyond the Beaverhead,[6] following the buffalo, elk, and deer. I was old enough to have my own root-digging stick,[7] old enough to scrape hides, old enough to be promised in marriage (about eleven snows) when the Minnetarees raided our summer camp at the Three Forks,[8] and I was taken.

I saw many of my people killed that day: four men, four women, most all of the boys. Some were able to escape into the trees. But me, they took, as they took most of the young girls.[9] So it was that I came to live as a slave among the Minnetarees at the village of Awatixa on the Big River Missouri.[10]

One day I found that my friend, Naya Nuki had escaped. I knew she would try to find our people. But the way was too long. The dangers were too many. I thought she would be recaptured and punished, or she would never find our people, and she would die. So I stayed.

I was made to work very hard. I learned to plant corn, beans, and squash.[11] I learned to tend the growing things and to harvest. I learned to mound up earth and trees in a big circle to make a lodge. And, I learned the language.

Lewis   July 28, 1805

"Our present camp is precisely on the spot that the Snake Indians were encamped at the time the Minnetarees of the Knife River first came in sight of them five years [ago]. From [here] they retreated about three miles up Jefferson's River and concealed themselves in the woods. The Minnetarees pursued, attacked them, killed four men, four women, a number of boys, and made prisoners of all the females. . . . Sah-cah-gar-we-ah, our Indian woman was one of the female prisoners taken at that time."

Awatixa *(ah-WAH-teek-sah)*
Camas *(KAM-us)*
Minnetarees *(min-eh-TAHR-eez)*
Naya Nuki *(nah-YAH nook-EH)*

Native Quillwork and Beadwork

As decorative glass beads became readily available, the popularity of ornamental quillwork declined. Porcupine quillwork was labor-intensive: the quills had to be soaked, flattened, and dyed, then folded and bent into patterns that would be sewn to leather. Beads, on the other hand, required only stringing and sewing. Bones, antlers, stones, shells, hooves, feathers, animal teeth, hair, and fur continued to be used as decoration after contact with non-natives.

Arikara *(ah-RIK-ah-rah)*
Assiniboine *(ah-SIN-eh-bwahn)*
Mandan *(MAN-dan)*

It was not an unbearable life. In many ways, it was better than the life I had known with my people. Here, there was always more food, less hunger.[12] Here, strange-looking and strange-sounding men from the trading companies[13] traveled up and down the Big River, bringing skins, iron cooking pots, corn grinders, ribbons and beads, axes, traps, and guns. They brought stories of what they had seen, and who they had traded with. Here, there were Mandan, Minnetaree (also called "Big Bellies"), Arikara, Assiniboine, Cree, and more.[14]

It was a life of interest. A life of plenty. I became content.

After a time, I was adopted into a Minnetaree clan and given a "woman's belt" made by the other women. Mine had blue beads on it, the sign of an industrious worker.[15] It was hoped I would marry into the tribe, for then my husband would be honor-bound to provide meat not only for me, but for the rest of my new clan. Such was the custom in those days.

Elkskin Shirt With Quillwork (Reproduction)

This leather shirt—a style adopted by the Corps of Discovery for its comfort and durability—shows the style and ornamentation typical of the Lewis-and-Clark-contact era. Porcupine quills have been dyed and sewn onto the shirt, and additional designs painted over the chest and arm sections. The long fringe was mostly ornamental but could be used as tying material if the necessity arose. A shirt like this would probably have taken two medium-sized hides to create. After brain tanning, the leather would have appeared very light in color, but often the leather was wood-smoked until it turned a yellowish color. The smoking process served two purposes: it overrode all scent of man, and it added oils and resins that served to waterproof the leather.

Headwaters of the Salmon River, Sawtooth National Recreation Area, Idaho

Midday Sun, Pretty Hidatsa Girl
Oil painting by George Catlin, 1832

Midday Sun could have been a contemporary of Sacagawea. As the painting seems to depict spring or summer, her dress is most likely made from deer or antelope hide. Extensive quillwork decorates the yoke and sleeves of the dress. The medallion design, fringed hem, and quilled leggings were typical of the Mandan and the Minnetaree. Midday Sun's ears are pierced in several places. It was not uncommon for both sexes to tattoo their bodies or to paint themselves with elaborate designs of vermillion and other mineral-based paints.

So how it was that I became the wife of a mixed-blood Frenchman,[16] I cannot say. Some say it was a game of chance. Some say a bet or a trade. In the end, it did not matter. It all turned out the same. Toussaint Charbonneau became my husband. (It was said of him that he was always marrying someone!) I was barely fourteen snows.

I moved into his lodge at the Second Village where I joined another of his wives and their son, also named Toussaint. Like me, Otter Woman was of the Snake tribe, but she was older than I. She had been with Charbonneau for many years.[17] I was glad there would be two of us in the lodge to share the work.

I wondered if Otter Woman still remembered the words of Numa, our birth people. But Charbonneau did not like to hear Shoshoni spoken. He could not understand the words. No! In his lodge, he told us, we would speak only the Minnetaree, or Hidatsa, such as he spoke, and the few words of French that he would teach us. That was all we needed to know.

Hidatsa *(hid-AHT-sah)*
Toussaint Charbonneau *(too-SAHN SHAR-bun-oh)*

Mandan Earth Lodge (Interior)

Engraving with aquatint by Karl Bodmer, circa 1839

Often measuring up to forty feet across, Mandan lodges provided ample space to stable horses and kennel dogs without encroaching upon human living space. The lodge also functioned as an informal meeting place, a workshop, nursery, kitchen, hotel, and storage facility. A central fire—ventilated through a smoke hole in the lodge roof—was screened from the entrance by upright logs, or puncheons, set in a trench for stability. The floor was tamped earth. Beds of buffalo robes were constructed to sit up off the floor, much like today's bed frames; many were enclosed by hides that hung from poles. The Mandan considered their lodges to belong to the women of the household.

**Bird's-Eye View of the Mandan Village
1800 Miles above St. Louis**

Oil painting by George Catlin, circa 1827–39

One of several along the Knife River at its juncture with the Missouri, this Mandan village would have felt familiar to Sacagawea. The related Minnetaree villages were close neighbors. The rounded, earth-mound lodges served not only to keep the weather out, but also as vantage points from which to view the village. (Note the groups of people on the roofs of their mounds.) Also on the roofs are "bull boats," so named for the bull buffalo hides stretched over willow frames to form the characteristic cup-like shape. An upright enclosure made of tree bark stood at the center of each village; this structure housed specific sacred objects. (See the enclosure at the center of this painting, flanked by four tall ceremonial poles.)

Morning fog hangs over an aspen stand in early autumn. Wasatch-Cache National Forest, Idaho.

When Lewis and Clark brought their men to our villages on the Big River, it was the time of the fallen leaves. Geese were already flying south. The smells of snow and warming fires were on the wind.

They smoked the pipe with the head men of all the tribes.[18] They made speeches and gave many gifts. Lights danced in the northern skies, which they took for a good sign, so they decided to stay through the winter.

They built rows of "houses," as they called them, made from "logs." But these houses sat flat against one another in straight lines, not rounded as a lodge should be . . . not round, as a village should be. Then they put up a high wall around their houses, closed the gate, and called it Fort Mandan.[19]

Clark   November 11, 1804

"A cold day. Continued to work at Fort [Mandan]. Two men cut themselves with an ax. . . . An Indian gave me several rolls of parched meat. Two squaws of the Rock[y] Mountains, purchased from the Indians by a Frenchman—Charbonneau—came down. The Mandans out hunting the buffalo."

Pehriska Ruhpa, Hidatsa Warrior
Engraving and aquatint by Karl Bodmer, circa 1839

Note the quillwork on the yoke of Pehriska Ruhpa's leather shirt and moccasins. The bold pattern on his buffalo robe was accomplished by quilling and/or painting. Around his neck sits a bear claw necklace, symbol of a hunter's skill and bravery. Pehriska Ruhpa holds his ceremonial pipe; it appears to be decorated with animal (and perhaps human) hair, beads, metal studs, and elaborate carving. Most pipes in this area were carved from red pipestone, or Catlinite.

Bunchberry, Meadow Creek roadless area,
Nez Perce National Forest, Idaho

We were all curious about the white men and what they kept inside the wall. It was said they had a big black dog, almost as big as a bear![20] And a big black man, almost as big as a tree! Charbonneau said his name was York. He was the slave of the red-haired chief, Clark. I thought this very strange, for no tribe I knew took men for slaves, only young women and girl children. The men, they killed, as befitted warriors. But Charbonneau said it was not the same with the whites.

The black man, York, was Big Medicine.[21] The chiefs of all the villages tried to rub the black off, like dirt. But it would not come off. Then they felt of his hair, which was rough like the hair of the buffalo.

"He is a different animal than the whites," they said. And all the People wanted to touch him, to be part of him and his Medicine.

Charbonneau said the white chiefs wanted to find a river way to the Big Water Where The Sun Goes Down.[22] They needed guides and interpreters to speak for them with those whose homelands they would cross. They would pay well. So Charbonneau began going to the fort every day to talk with one of their interpreters who spoke French.

Clark   October 9, 1804

"*The Indians much astonished at my black servant, and call him Big Medicine. . . . [He] did not lose the opportunity of displaying his power, strength, etc., etc. . . . [which] made him look more terrible than we wished him to be. . . . This nation never saw a black man before.*"

Then one day, Charbonneau told Otter Woman and me that he would be going with Lewis and Clark and their men when they left in the spring. We should begin making more moccasins and clothing for him, for he would be gone a very long time—longer than he had ever been gone before.[23]

He questioned us about our birth people, the Snakes. Where was their homeland? Would they be friendly to the whites? Did they have horses as he had heard? And, could we trade with them for those horses so we could cross the Shining Mountains?[24]

Otter Woman came from a different band than mine.[25] It had been many snows since she had seen them, or even thought about them. But my people, Agui Dika, lived where Lewis and Clark wanted to go. Yes, I knew they had horses. Would they trade? This I did not know, for trading horses was something the men did, not the women.

And I could not say if they would be friendly to the whites. They had never seen one before, as far as I knew. I had not . . . not until I came here, to the Big River.[26]

Willow Fish Weir

The fish weir, or trap, was constructed from thin willow branches that were secured by twining around the "hoops" and nose. The weir was generally placed in the water with the open end against the current, unless it was spawning time. At that time—because the fish swam against the current to reach their spawning grounds—the weir was placed in the water, open end with the current. The weir's operating principle relied on the fish swimming into the opening to be trapped by the current against the weir's nose. The weir was then scooped out of the water.

Agui Dika (*ah-GUY-dee-kah*)

Black Moccasin, Aged Chief
Oil Painting by George Catlin, 1832

Black Moccasin was a chief in the associated Minnetaree-Mandan villages when Lewis and Clark lived there through the winter of 1804-5. Wrapped in a buffalo robe (hair side inward) that features typical Minnetaree-Mandan quillwork, the chief holds his ceremonial pipe. His shield, quiver of arrows, feather headdress, and a buffalo horn headdress sit nearby.

Then Charbonneau asked if I remembered the words, the words of Agui Dika—Shoshoni. Could I speak them again? It had been so long since I had been allowed to speak them! But, oh yes, I remembered.

"Then you will come with me!" Charbonneau ordered. "Your people will speak to you in Shoshoni. You will say the words to me in Hidatsa, and I will say the words to someone else in French. Then that man will say the words in English for Lewis and Clark to understand."[27]

I did not want to go. I was big and slow and awkward—with child. I did not know when the baby would come.

Charbonneau said it did not matter. A woman with a baby would be a good sign. It would show, at a glance, that the Corps of Discovery was not a war party. Then he told me to gather our belongings. We were moving inside the fort.

He said nothing about Otter Woman and their son, Toussaint, coming with us. We knew, by his silence, they would be left behind for our Minnetaree relatives to look after.

Palisade at Fort Mandan (Reconstruction)

Fort Mandan was laid out on a triangular pattern, the base of which formed the entrance wall. Living quarters adjoined one another on both sides of the triangle, meeting in back at the point where a guard tower was constructed. Each room likely contained a crude fireplace.

When my time for birthing came, the pains started in the night. Lewis and Clark had ordered the gates of Fort Mandan closed every night at sundown and kept barred until morning. So Otter Woman was not with me to help bring the baby. The labor was long and hard. I was exhausted by the pain. I thought I might not live to see morning if the baby did not come soon.

Finally, someone sent for Lewis. He and Clark had been making medicine on many in the villages throughout the winter. Maybe there was something in his pills and powders for me? But no, not for childbirth.[28]

Then the interpreter Jussome, whose family lived in the Mandan village,[29] said the rattle of a snake would make the baby come.

"Break it between your fingers," he told Lewis, "then make her drink."

I drank. Within minutes, my son was born!

"His name will be Jean Baptiste," shouted Charbonneau. "Named after my father!"[30]

But to me, my son would always be Pomp, meaning "first-born" in the language of Agui Dika.

Thomas Jefferson's Medicine Chest

The "walnut chest," listed in Lewis's inventory as a repository for medical supplies, was probably very much like this one belonging to President Jefferson. Lewis had likely seen this chest during his tenure at Monticello as Jefferson's personal secretary. Later, while under the tutelage of Dr. Benjamin Rush, he no doubt saw a variety of medical kits. Though Jefferson's kit shows a good number of glass bottles with stoppers, Lewis's Expedition inventory indicates only three, eight-ounce, stopped bottles. The odds of glass breakage were much higher on his journey than at Monticello with Mr. Jefferson. Lewis tried to anticipate quantities and kinds of medicines sufficient for a two-year military expedition. He acquired teas, powdered barks, heavy oils, powdered minerals in oils and salts, gum camphor, opiates in various bases, mercury (widely used in the treatment of venereal disease), menthol, and fifty dozen of Dr. Benjamin Rush's "bilious pills," commonly called thunder pills because of the sudden and copious evacuation that resulted from taking them. Lewis laid in emetics and purgatives, plasters, douches, and exotic spices. A set of small pocket instruments, syringes, lancets for "bleeding," lint for bandaging, and gum elastic for binding round out the list.

Lewis   February 11, 1805

"About five o'clock this evening one of the wives of Charbonneau was delivered of a fine boy. . . . her labor was tedious and the pain violent. Mr. Jussome informed me that he had frequently administered a small portion of the rattle of the rattlesnake, which he assured me had never failed to produce . . . hastening the birth of the child. Having the rattle of a snake . . .
I gave it to him and he administered two rings of it to the woman, broken in small pieces with the fingers and added to a small quantity of water. . . .
Perhaps this remedy may be worthy of future experiments . . ."

Mandan Dog Sled on Ice
Engraving by Karl Bodmer, circa 1839.

In the Mandan and Minnetaree societies, dogs were meant to work. When the rivers froze over in the winter, dog sleds pulled people and provisions over the ice. The Mandan woman in this engraving is also burdened; like the sled dogs, Mandan women were expected to be burden-carriers

The next moon, ice began to snap and crack on the river. It was no longer safe to walk across the ice between the villages. I finished the cradleboard of willows I was making for Pomp. A few weeks more, and the river was flowing free. It was time to leave.

The long, flat canoes–called pirogues–were loaded with as many goods as they could carry: boxes, bundles of papers, instruments, books.[31] There was barely enough room to sit.[32] Sometimes Lewis's dog would run along the riverbank. Sometimes he would swim. Sometimes he would try to climb inside the boats! I carried Pomp in the cradleboard, or in a sling made of skins, on my back.[33]

Lewis April 22, 1805

"I ascended to the top of the cut bluff this morning, from whence I had a most delightful view [of]. . . immense herds of buffalo, elk, deer, and antelope feeding in one common and boundless pasture. We saw a number of beaver. . . several of which we shot. Found them large and fat. . . Walking on shore this evening, I met with a buffalo calf which attached itself to me, and continued to follow close at my heels until I embarked and left it. It appeared alarmed at my dog. . . Captain Clark informed me that he saw a large drove of buffalo pursued by wolves today. . . The cows only defend their young so long as they are able to keep up with the herd, and seldom return any distance in search of them."

pirogue *(pee-ROAG)*

Pronghorn Antelope

Lewis and Clark frequently mention the game they observed and killed along their journey. In one journal entry, Lewis writes that Seaman, his huge dog, drowned an antelope in the river, then dragged it to camp for the men to butcher. Antelope (or "goats" as they were sometimes called in the journals) are very fleet and agile creatures. If the animals have not been run a long time before they are killed and field dressed, their meat is quite sweet in taste. The hooves of the antelope were often used as rattles or in ornamentation; the horns were sometimes used in ceremony. Since their leather is very supple and light-weight, antelope hides were often made into spring and summer clothing.

Prairie Dog

On the same day Sacagawea, Pomp, and Charbonneau embarked west with the Corps of Discovery, boats were sent east with specimens and documents bound for President Jefferson. One of those specimens was a live prairie dog in a cage. Scientifically known as *Cynomys ludovicianus,* black tailed prairie dogs were first described in a very long and detailed journal entry of September 7, 1804 as "barking squirrels." The live specimen sent to President Jefferson by Lewis and Clark survived, providing much amusement at Monticello.

Traditional Shoshoni Cradleboard

This cradleboard frame is made from willows and covered with hide. The distinctive willow visor could be covered with rabbit fur in winter (as shown), or kept open in summer to shade the infant's face. Cradleboards were typically carried on the mother's back, either with a chest band or a band across her forehead, but they could also be leaned up against a tree or rock by means of the rest, or "foot" section. The style of cradleboard that Sacagawea would have made for Pomp is unknown.

Lewis   May 24-25, 1805

"It happened, unfortunately for us this evening, that Charbonneau was at the helm of the pirogue [again . . . and] equally unlucky that Captain Clark and myself were both on shore at that moment. . . . In this pirogue were embarked our papers, instruments, books, medicine . . . in short, almost every article indispensably necessary to . . . ensure the success of the enterprise in which we are now launched to the distance of 2,200 miles. . . . Suffice it to say . . . a sudden squall . . . struck [the pirogue] and instantly upset [it] and would have turned her completely topsy-turvy had it not been for the resistance made by the [sail] against the water. . . . Charbonneau, still crying to his God for mercy, had not yet recollected the rudder . . . [nor could anyone] bring him to his [senses] until [Cruzatte] threatened to shoot him instantly if he did not take hold of the rudder and do his duty. . . .

"The Indian woman, to whom I ascribe equal fortitude and resolution with any person on board at the time of the accident, caught and preserved most of the light articles which were washed overboard. . . ."

The men took turns with the boats, even Charbonneau who could not swim.[34] He was steering our boat when the wind gusted against us so hard, it almost tipped us over. If the sail had not caught on the water, we all would have been thrown into the river. Waves spilled over the side, into the boat.

Two of the men started scooping water out of the boat with kettles. Three others tried to row us to the bank. Pomp was safe on my back. Then I saw things start to float away, down the river. I did what anyone would do; I grabbed them as they passed me and pulled them back into the boat. A few things of great weight sank, but in the end, very little was lost.

One day went into the next . . . and the next . . . and the next. The men killed buffalo, antelope, and bear. The big dog was bitten on the leg by a beaver and almost died, but Lewis worked his medicine on the wound and the dog lived.

Obsidian Knife and Sheath

Even before the arrival of missionaries among the tribes, the "cross" design was popular. Generally, this design signified the Four Directions, or symbolized stars, depending upon the tribe of origin. Both men and women routinely wore knives.

A deep water-filled glacial kettle sits amidst the grassy, glacial plain on the western slope of the Wind River Mountains, Bridger Wilderness, Bridger-Teton National Forest, Wyoming.

Lewis August 17, 1805

"We next inquired who were chiefs among them. . . . We gave him a medal of the small size with the likeness of Mr. Jefferson, the President of the United States, in relief on one side, and clasped hands with a pipe and tomahawk on the other. To the other chiefs we gave each a small medal which [was] struck in the presidency of George Washington, Esquire. We also gave small medals of the last description to two young men who. . . were good young men and much respected among [the tribe]."

Chief of the Blood Indians (Detail)
Engraving with aquatint by Karl Bodmer, circa 1839

This Blood chief wears one of the Jefferson peace medals around his neck. The largest of a variety of peace medals (such as this one) were usually reserved for those individuals Lewis and Clark deemed most important within a region or tribe. Some medals were silver; others, bronze. The captains also dispensed peace medals with George Washington on the face, farming scenes on the reverse, and special US silver dollars outfitted with rings at the top for ease in stringing.

Jefferson Peace Medal, Face and Reverse (Reproduction)

This particular piece shows the profile of President Thomas Jefferson on the face, with the inscription, "TM. JEFFERSON PRESIDENT OF THE U.S. A.D.1801." The back of the medal shows a tomahawk and (peace) pipe above two clasped hands. The inscription reads, "PEACE AND FRIENDSHIP."

We stopped with many tribes where the men would smoke their pipes and say their speeches. They talked about the Great Father Jefferson and the need for peace. They gave medals like the one they had given to me, with the face of the Great Father on one side and two hands clasping on the other.[35] It was said that two hands clasped in friendship could not be raised against one another in war.

They traded for buckskins, parfleches, quillwork, and shields to take back to the Great Father. They pulled out their writing desks and made marks in their journals.[36] Each day brought us closer to the Shining Mountains and the need for horses.

Soon, the captains grew anxious. Each time we would find the remains of a camp, or the sign of a party that had passed, they would ask Charbonneau, "Are these her people? Are these the Snakes?"

Lap Desk with Ink Powder and Quill Pen

Journal writing would have been a laborious task. Ink powder first had to be mixed with water, and the entries written with quill pens. Only certain quills maintained their shape when cut to a pen "nib"; goose quills were considered the best. Lap desks of this period were hinged between lid and base so they could lie flat to provide an adequate writing surface. A storage compartment in the base held writing supplies and a small knife to sharpen quill nibs.

Parfleche
(Columbia Plateau Style)

The parfleche or animal hide suitcase—was in use by native peoples far before the advent of the Corps of Discovery. The hide's hair was singed off with fire and the hide scraped with hand tools until smooth. After proper curing, the resulting leather was shaped and decorated with mineral paints. Spread flat and open, the parfleche (a French word meaning "of skin") could accommodate a number of items. The sides were then folded in and tied. Finally, the ends were folded over and those, too, were tied.

parfleche (*pahr-FLESH*)

"The dimensions of the cache are in proportion to the quantity of articles intended to be deposited. As the earth is dug, it is . . . carefully laid on a skin or cloth, and then carried to someplace where it can be thrown in such manner as to conceal it. . . . Before the goods are deposited, they must be well dried . . . [with] a parcel of small dry sticks . . . a floor is made, three or four inches thick, which is then covered with some dry hay or rawhide, well dried. On this, the articles are deposited, taking care to keep them from touching the walls by putting other dry sticks between as you stow away the merchandise. When nearly full, the goods are covered with a skin, and earth thrown in and well rammed, until—with the addition of the turf first removed—the hole is on a level with the surface of the ground. In this manner, dried skins or merchandise will keep perfectly sound for several years."

Sage Grouse

Near the place of the Buffalo Jump[37] they found worn-out moccasins in a deserted camp site, and had me "read" them. No, these were not the shape or decoration of the Agui Dika.

The way grew harder. Holes, called caches, were dug in the ground. Here, the white men buried supplies so their loads would be lighter. They pulled the canoes with ropes wrapped over their shoulders. Sometimes we carried the burdens on our backs–even the captains.

I thought the great black dog would be made to pack supplies, too, but this did not happen. He helped bring down game for us to eat, and barked at strange noises in the night which woke us to danger, but I never saw him work in the way dogs were expected to work at the Mandan villages. Lewis, especially, treated him with much affection.

Trade Beads

cache *(cash)*

The way grew harder still. Our feet were cut and bruised by stones. Sharp spines pierced our skin, even through our moccasins. Then, at the Time of the Long Grass, I began to be sick.[38] At first I felt heavy and dull. Then came the fever. Lewis cut me, trying to bleed the sickness from me. But it did no good. Then he wrapped me in poultices of tree bark and made me drink opium tea.

For days I was out of my head, walking among the spirits. My heart would race, then slow to nothing, then race again. My hands and arms trembled like leaves in a storm.

Finally, Lewis made me drink water from a stinking spring.

"Sulphur," he said. Again and again, he made me drink until I slept. The next morning, I woke. I knew who I was. And, I was hungry!

Lewis   June 3, 1805

"Those who have remained in camp today have been busily engaged in dressing skins for clothing. . . . Many of them have their feet so mangled and bruised with the stones and rough ground over which they passed barefoot, that they can scarcely walk or stand. . . . It is with great pain they do either. For some days past, they were unable to wear their moccasins."

Statue of Seaman, Lewis's Dog, in Seaside, OR

Lewis's faithful Newfoundland dog is immortalized in this Oregon monument, which stands near the location of Lewis and Clark's Pacific Ocean salt works. Equally at home in water or on land, the Newfoundland breed is well known for its strength, endurance, intelligence, and sweet disposition. Although its heavy double coat is water resistant and provides extra protection from sun and insects, Lewis's journal entries for the spring of 1805 describe the mosquitoes as being so bad that, "My dog even howls with the torture he experiences from them." Seaman stood guard in camp at night, brought down wild game, provided distracting antics for trail-weary travelers, and became a much-loved "member" of the Expedition.

Clark   *June 11, 1805*

"The Indian woman very sick. I bled her, which appeared to be of great service to her."

Lewis   *June 16, 1805*

"The Indian woman extremely ill and much reduced by her indisposition. This gave me some concern . . . for the poor object herself, then with a young child in her arms, [and also for] her being our only dependence for a friendly negotiation with the Snake Indians on whom we depend for horses to assist . . . our portage from the Missouri to the Columbia River."

Lewis   *June 19, 1805*

"The Indian woman was much better this morning [but] she walked out and gathered a considerable amount of the white apples . . . which she [ate] so heartily in their raw state (together with a considerable quantity of dried fish, [all] without my knowledge) that she complained very much, and her fever returned. I rebuked Charbonneau severely for [allowing] her to indulge herself with such food, [as he had been] previously told what she must only eat. I now gave her broken doses of diluted nitre[tonic] until it produced perspiration, and at 10 P.M., 30 drops of laudanum which gave her a tolerable night's rest."

But they fed me only buffalo broth, saying I had almost died. They said I was too weak for food. One day passed, then two days. Still, only buffalo broth with a few tiny pieces of meat to eat. I asked again and again for more.

On the third day, I was still hungry. So I waited until no one was looking, and I slipped away from camp. I found some bread-root to dig. "Prairie apples" they are called.[39] Even though I knew they were not ready for digging, I ate them anyway. I ate and ate and ate and ate, until I was no longer hungry.

That night my stomach thundered and I was in terrible pain. My fever returned. Lewis was very angry.

"Too many raw apples, Janey! And too little sense!"

Once I was stronger, we began the long, hard climb around the Great Thundering Falls. The men put a sail on one of the canoes. The wind blew against it so hard, the canoe raced along on its wheels just as if it had been on water. Sailing on dry land, they called it.

Arrowheads

Great Falls of the Missouri River, Montana

The Corps of Discovery would have heard the deafening roar of the Great Falls of the Missouri from many miles away, but they were completely unprepared for the sight of it days later. Lewis rhapsodized about the falls in his journal; he was not the last to do so. Before the river was dammed, many viewers were either struck dumb or lifted to emotional ecstasy at first sight of the Great Falls. Unfortunately, the visually sublime was also the physically excruciating. The long portage of canoes and supplies demanded by the Great Falls was almost the Corps's undoing.

Hand-Hewn Canoe

Precisely the type of canoe (pirogue) used by the Corps of Discovery, this canoe was large enough to accomodate ten adults or an abundance of cargo. It sat low in the water and could achieve respectable speeds. Off the water, however, the canoe had to be pulled by the men using "trucks" (or wheeled frames) and muscle power. At one point, the men hoisted a sail in one of the canoes and let the wind carry it over the flat, dry land.

Clark *July 29, 1805*

"I determined to proceed on to the falls, and take the river. I took my servant and one man. Charbonneau . . . and his squaw accompanied. Soon after I arrived at the falls, I perceived a cloud which appeared black and threatened immediate rain. I looked . . . for a shelter but could see no place without being in great danger of being blown into the river if the wind should prove as turbulent as it is at some times. About 1/4 of a mile above the falls, I observed a deep ravine in which were shelving rocks under which we took shelter. . . . Placed our guns, the compass, etc., under a shelving rock on the upper side of the creek in a place which was very secure from the rain. . . . Soon after, a torrent of rain and hail fell more violent than ever I saw before. The rain fell like one volley of water falling from the heavens. . . . [It] gave us time only to get out of the way of a torrent of water which was pouring down the hill into the river with immense force, tearing everything before it, taking with it large rocks and mud.

"I took my gun and shot pouch in my left hand and with the right, scrambled up the hill, pushing the interpreter's wife (who had her child in her arms) before me. The interpreter, himself, [made] attempts to pull up his wife by the hand, [who was] much scared and nearly without motion. We at length reached the top of the hill safely, where I found my servant in search of us, greatly agitated for our welfare.

"Before I got out of the bottom of the ravine, which was flat, dry rock when I entered it, the water was up to my waist and wet my watch. I scarcely got out before it rose 10 feet deep with a torrent which was terrible to behold. And by the time I reached the top of the hill, [there was] at least 15 feet of water. I directed the party to return to the camp [on a] run as fast as possible . . . where our clothes could be [fetched] to cover the child (whose clothes were all lost), and the woman (who was . . . just recovering from a severe indisposition and was wet and cold). I was fearful of [her] relapse. I caused her . . . [and the rest of the] party to take a little spirits, which my servant had in a canteen. . . . [This] revived them very much."

Then the storms came. They battered and bruised us. Hailstones the size of fists slammed down from the sky, knocking some senseless and tearing our clothes to rags.[40] The sky grew black. It boiled. The wind howled like wolves.

Clark, Charbonneau, and I took shelter in a ravine, thinking the overhanging rocks would keep us dry. I took the cradleboard from my back and took Pomp out. I clutched him to me, pressing us hard against the dirt bank. But the rain came too hard and fast. The hillsides suddenly gave way in a torrent of water, rocks, and mud.

Charbonneau got out first, then reached down for me. Clark was standing waist-deep in water, where no water had been before. He pushed me up to Charbonneau with Pomp in my arms. Clark barely had time to scramble up behind me before the water was as tall as two men, then three. We lost the cradleboard, but my Pomp was safe.[41]

Later, Clark wrote of this in his journal. He named the place "Defeated Drain."

Clark   *August 1, 1806*

"I was obliged to land to let the buffalo cross over. . . . This gang of buffalo was entirely across [the river channel] and as thick as they could swim. . . . The channel on the side of the island [where] they went into the river was crowded with animals for half an hour . . . . the other side of the island, for more than 3/4 of an hour. . . . [Later that day] two gangs of buffalo crossed a little below us, as numerous as the first."

Lewis   *May 29, 1805*

"Today we passed . . . the remains of a vast many mangled carcasses of buffalo which had been driven over a precipice of 120 feet by the Indians, and had perished. The water appeared to have washed away a part of this pile of slaughter, and still there remained the fragments of at least a hundred carcasses. They created a most horrid stench. In this manner the Indians of the Missouri destroy vast herds of buffalo at a stroke. For this purpose, one of the most active and fleet young men is selected [then] disguised in a robe of buffalo skin (having also the . . . buffalo's head with the ears and horns fastened on, in the form of a cap). . . . He places himself at a convenient distance between a herd of buffalo and a precipice. . . . The other Indians now surround the herd on the back and flanks, and at a signal . . . all show themselves at the same time moving forward toward the buffalo. The disguised Indian (or decoy) has taken care to place himself sufficiently [near] the buffalo to be noticed by them when they take to flight, and running before them, they follow him in full speed to the precipice. The [buffalo] behind [drive] those in front over [the bluff], and seeing them go down, do not look or hesitate about following. . . . The decoy in the meantime, has taken care to secure himself in some cranny or crevice of the cliff which he had previously prepared for that purpose. The part of the decoy . . . is extremely dangerous. If they are not very fleet runners, the buffalo tread them underfoot and crush them to death, and sometimes drive them over the precipice also, where they perish in common with the buffalo."

The Beaverhead Mountains and Birch Creek Valley, Clark County, Idaho

We traveled on. Slowly, I began to recognize the country. We stopped at the Three Forks where I had been taken from my people by the Minnetaree. Then I spotted the Beaverhead Hill. I knew we were getting closer to the Agui Dika.

But many of the men were sick or injured. Lewis decided he and a few of the others would go on ahead and try to find my people. I thought Charbonneau and I would be allowed to go with him, since I knew the talk. Lewis said no, Clark and the rest of us would stay here until all could follow.[42]

First though, Lewis wanted to know what was the word for white man in Shoshoni. There wasn't one.

Instead I told Charbonneau, "Tell him ta-vai-bon-e,"[43] which meant the same as "stranger." It was as close a word as I could think of.

Lewis August 11, 1805

"When I had arrived within about a mile, [the Shoshone tribesman] made a halt, which I did also. . . . Unloosing my blanket from my pack, I made him the signal of friendship known to the Indians of the Rocky Mountains and those of Missouri—which is, by holding the mantle or robe in your hands at two corners, and then throwing it up in the air higher than the head [and] bringing it to earth as if in the act of spreading it [then] repeating three times. . . . This signal had not the desired effect.

"I now called to him in as loud a voice as I could command, repeating the word tab-ba-bone which in their language signifies 'white man.' . . . I again repeated the word tab-ba-bone and held up trinkets in my hands, and stripped up my shirt sleeve to give him an opportunity of seeing the color of my skin, and advanced leisurely toward him. But he did not remain . . . [and] suddenly turned his horse about, gave him the whip, leaped the creek, and disappeared in the willow brush in an instant. . . . With him vanished all my hopes of obtaining horses for the present."

Woman of the Snake Tribe (Detail)

Engraving with aquatint, vignette from Tableau 33, by Swiss artist Karl Bodmer from his journeys among the Plains tribes in 1833.

This Shoshone woman wears her hair loose in typical Shoshone fashion. A traditional Shoshone dress was made from brain-tanned deer or elk hide; deer hide was for warm weather, elk hide for cold. Each dress took five to seven deer hides, or three to four elk hides. Typical ornamentation included mineral paint designs, dyed porcupine quills (and later, beads), animal teeth and hair, and shells. For ceremonial wear, the ensemble would have also included decorated leggings, quilled or beaded moccasins, a belt, and sometimes a breastplate made of bone.

One of the men going with Lewis knew the sign talk, so he could make himself understood. Lewis, himself, knew to make the welcome signals with his blanket, waving it in the air, then spreading it on the ground as if for trade or council.

I told Charbonneau, "Tell him to paint the cheeks of the women red, as a sign of peace." Then they were gone.[44]

It was more than seven suns before we caught up to them. I will never forget entering into the camp of the Agui Dika. First, I smelled the smoke of the tanning fires. Then, I heard the familiar sounds of dogs barking and children laughing. I danced with excitement and sucked my fingers to tell Clark these were, indeed, the people of my childhood.

The dogs ran out to meet us first, snarling and yelping and sniffing at our ankles. Then came the proud, young men. Finally came the women with their children. Lewis and the head men of the camp strode forward. They embraced Clark so many times, soon all were smeared with grease and paint. "The national hug," Lewis called it.

Lewis August 13, 1805

"These [Shoshone] men then advanced and embraced me very affectionately in their way, which is by putting their left arm over your right shoulder [and] clasping your back, while they apply their left cheek to yours, and frequently [exclaim] the word ah-hi-e, ah-hi-e . . . [or] 'I am much pleased; I am much rejoiced'. . . . We were all caressed and besmeared with their grease and paint until I was heartily tired of the national hug."

The women closed around me.

"Sai! Sai!" they sang, "Ah-hi-e! It is good."

I held my son out to them.

"Behold the faces of your grandmothers," I told Pomp. "Numa. These are The People."

My eyes went from one face to another. Then I saw her. No, it could not be! But then she smiled. There could be no mistake. Naya Nuki! My friend! She was alive! She had found our people after all! We clung to one another's necks and cried and cried and cried. We had both survived.

The men went off together. We women did the same, talking all at once and touching one another. It had been so long since I had heard this much Shoshoni spoken at one time, I do not remember now all that was said.

All too soon, Charbonneau sent for me. It was time to talk about getting horses for crossing the Shining Mountains.

Lewis   August 17, 1805

"The meeting of [Sacagawea with her people] was really affecting, particularly between Sah-cah-gar-we-ah and an Indian woman who had been taken prisoner at the same time with her, and who had afterwards escaped from the Minnetarees and rejoined her nation."

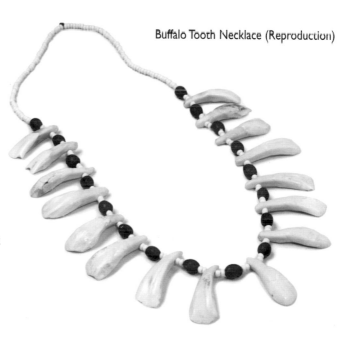

Buffalo Tooth Necklace (Reproduction)

Bitterroot in Bloom

The bitterroot lives up to its name, but is still considered one of the most important roots gathered by the mountain tribes. The roots must be dug carefully from their usually rocky soil, and the thin stringers painstakingly traced to their ends well beneath the ground's surface. The roots are then dried, cut, or pounded, for use in medicine, food, or ceremony.

ah-hi-e *(AH-hi-eh)*
Sai *(sigh)*

Lewis   August 17, 1805

"Here . . . we formed a canopy of one of our large sails and planted some willow brush in the ground to form a shade for the Indians to sit under while we spoke to them, which we thought best to do this evening. Accordingly, we called them together and through the [translations] of LaBiche, Charbonneau, and Sah-cah-gar-we-ah, we communicated to them fully the [objectives] which had brought us into this distant part of the country. . . . [We] apprized them of the strength of our government and its friendly dispositions toward them. We also [said] we wished to penetrate the country as far as the ocean to the west [in order to] find a more direct way to bring merchandise to them. . . . [We told them] that as no trade could be [carried on with them] before our return to our homes . . . it was mutually advantageous to them [and] ourselves that they should render us [whatever] aids . . . they had it in their power to furnish, in order to hasten our voyage . . . [such as] horses to carry our baggage (without which we could not subsist), and . . . a guide to conduct us through the mountains."

It was unusual for a woman to speak in Council, so I wrapped my blanket around me as I entered and kept my eyes down, showing respect. I took off my moccasins and tucked my legs under me, to the right, so my dress covered them, for modesty, in the old way.

First, Lewis spoke. The words were repeated in French, then Charbonneau said them in Hidatsa to me. I said them in Shoshoni, and waited for a reply.

The one Lewis called "Chief" started to talk. I knew that voice! My head jerked up and I stared into his face. I knew I should not do this, but I could not help myself.

"Brother!"

I jumped to my feet and reached to clasp my blanket around us both, reclaiming my clan. I wept openly now.

"Brother! Brother!"[45]

Even in my joy, I was afraid I had shamed him—first, crying out in Council—then, showing so much feeling in front of the men. But Cameahwait's eyes showed no anger to me, only surprise. Now, emotion flowed over me like a river too big for its banks. I could barely sit through the rest of the Council.

Coyote Pelt

Known by a variety of names by different tribes, the coyote (or prairie wolf) played a key role in storytelling and moral instruction.

Cameahwait *(kah-MAY-ah-wait)*
LaBiche *(la-BEESH)*

Tools

The obsidian-bladed knife (a reproduction at left) has an elk antler handle. The projectile and blade point have been hand-formed from chert, flint, and agate. Today, artifacts found on public lands are protected by the federal Antiquities Act of 1906, and the Historical Sites Act of 1966; both prohibit individual collection. The projectile and blade point shown here were found on private land.

In the end, Lewis and Clark got the horses they needed for crossing the mountains. And I got my family back. So many were now dead: mother, father, sisters. But one of my sisters had left a son. I adopted him that day, as was our custom. He became my son, and I became his mother. So it would be, from that time forward.[46]

Yet I almost got more family than I wanted. The man my father had promised me to in marriage, as a child, now came forward to claim me as his wife! He already had two wives, so when he saw I had Pomp, he decided he did not want me so badly after all. I think he did not want another small mouth to feed.

Beaded Shoshone Moccasins

Each tribe had its own moccasin style. The pair shown here is of typical Shoshone construction and design, circa 1900.

Long Canyon Creek flows past a stand of old-growth western red cedar and white pine trees, Selkirk Mountains, Kanisku National Forest, Idaho.

Lewis   *August 13, 1805*

"Drouillard, who had had a good view of their horses, estimated them at 400. Most of them are fine horses; indeed, many of them would make a [fine] figure on the south side of the James River [back home] . . . [in the] land of fine horses. I saw several with Spanish brands on them, and some mules, which they informed me . . . they had also obtained from the Spaniards. I also saw a bridle bit of Spanish make and sundry other articles, which I have no doubt were obtained from the same source. . . . Each warrior keeps one or more horses tied by a cord to a stake near his lodge both day and night, and are always prepared for action at a moment's warning. They fight on horseback altogether. I observe that the large [biting] flies are extremely troublesome to the horses, as well as [to] ourselves."

Lewis   *July 21, 1805*

"We see daily great numbers of geese with their young, which are perfectly feathered except for the wings, which are deficient in both young and old. My dog caught several today, as he frequently does."

Lewis   August 16, 1805

"Neither the Indians nor ourselves had anything to eat . . . [then] one of the white men . . . killed a deer. . . . When [the Shoshone] arrived where the deer was . . . they dismounted and ran in, tumbling over each other like a parcel of famished dogs, each seizing and tearing away a part of the intestines which had been previously thrown out by Drouillard, who had killed it. . . . Each one had a piece of some description, and all were eating most ravenously. Some were eating the kidney, the [reproductive glands], the liver, and the blood [was] running from the corners of their mouths. . Others were in a similar situation with the paunch and guts. . . . One . . . had provided himself with about nine feet of the small guts, one end of which he was chewing on while with his hands, he was squeezing the contents out of the other. . . . I viewed these poor starved devils with pity and compassion. I directed McNeal to skin the deer and reserved a quarter. The balance, I gave to the chief to be divided among his people. They devoured the whole of it . . . without cooking. . . . Drouillard had killed a second deer . . . [where] nearly the same scene was enacted. . . . We cooked and ate [our portion] and gave the balance of the two deer to the Indians, who ate the whole of them, even to the soft parts of the hooves."

My people were starving. Game had become so scarce, they ate animals raw at the kill site, right down to the soft part of the hooves! The women dug all the roots and gathered all the berries they could find, but it was not enough. It was past time for my people to follow the buffalo. They had stayed at this camp out of respect for Lewis and Clark. Now, they could wait no longer.

And now, our path led in the other direction, across the Shining Mountains to the river the whites called "Columbia," and from there to the Big Water Where The Sun Goes Down. We traveled on. I did not know when, if ever, I would see the Agui Dika again.[47]

Mule Deer Buck and Doe

Named by Lewis and Clark for their enormous ears, these mule deer were larger than those hunted by the Corpsmen in the eastern United States. With the hair left on, mule deer hides made excellent blankets; with the hair off, very supple, light-to-medium weight leather. When old manuscripts and books speak of "buckskin" or "doeskin," they generally refer to the tanned hide of a deer. Deer are larger than antelope; therefore, they yield more meat. Also called venison, mule deer meat is stronger in taste than either antelope or elk meat, but like them, it is high in protein and very low in fat.

Nez Perce *(nez-purs)*
Nimiipu *(nee-ME-pooh)*
Wetkuiis *(WET-koo-ees)*

Day followed day, and we began to endure what my people had endured. There was less and less game. Before, it had taken four deer every day, or an elk and a deer, or a buffalo to feed us. Now, there was next to nothing. The parched corn[48] and "carry-soup"[49] of Captain Lewis could not sustain us without meat. So the white men started killing the horses to eat, the same horses they had bargained so hard for, with my brother. Later, they traded for dogs and ate them.

I refused, no matter how hungry I was. Numa do not eat their dogs or their horses![50]

When we came to the Nez Perce (Nimiipu), they fed us well. It was said that at first they had decided to kill us, or let us die of our own ignorance. But an old woman among them, whose name was Wetkuiis, said white traders had one time saved her life.[51] She said now the tribe should spare ours, so the debt would be balanced. Because of her words, the Nimiipu welcomed us.[52] They honored us. They traded many goods.

Clark   September 14, 1805

"Crossed a very high, steep mountain for 9 miles. . . . We crossed Glade Creek [where the] Indians have made 2 weirs across [the creek] to catch salmon . . . but . . . I could see no [evidence of] fish. . . . We were compelled to kill a colt for our men and [our]selves to eat, for the want of meat and we named the south fork [of the river we camped upon] Colt Killed Creek."

Clark   October 18, 1805

"We thought it necessary to lay in a store of provisions for our voyage, and the fish being out of season, we purchased 40 dogs, for which we have articles of little value such as bells, thimbles, knitting pins, brass wire, and a few beads—all of which they appeared well satisfied and pleased."

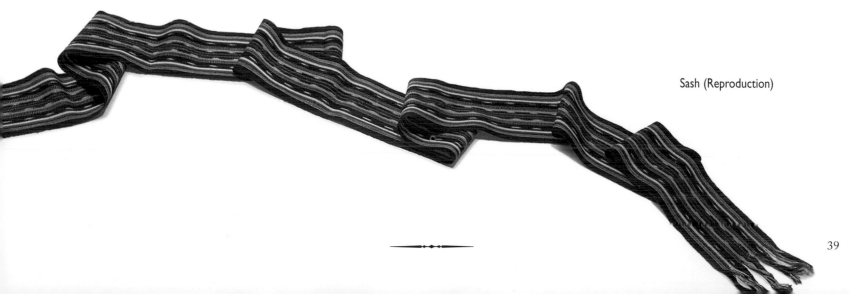

Sash (Reproduction)

The chief, Twisted Hair,[53] drew a map on white elk skin of the rivers flowing west. It was decided to leave our horses with Twisted Hair's band until we came back from the Big Water. Lewis told his men to start building canoes.

Word traveled fast of our coming once we were back on the rivers. Drumming and singing followed us down to the Columbia, then toward the Big Water. Sometimes the man Cruzatte played his fiddle in return, though it sounded more like a wounded animal than music.

Bitterroot Mountains from Friday Ridge, Selway Bitterroot Wilderness Area, Clearwater National Forrest, Idaho

American Beaver

The beaver triggered an opportunistic onslaught of the American wilderness. On the heels of the Lewis and Clark Expedition, trappers found a seemingly inexhaustible supply of beaver whose pelts became almost worth their weight in gold.

Artist's Field Kit

Though this kit dates to the 1850s, the design had not changed in over a century; Lewis and Clark would have recognized it immediately. Clark was the primary artist of the Expedition, though both captains did extensive sketching in their journals. Paints, papers, brushes, mixing dishes, and blotting pads are included in this field kit. Both George Catlin and Karl Bodmer, artists who first painted the native peoples of the Lewis and Clark route, used boxes such as this one.

Clark   November 7, 1805

"Great joy in camp. We are in view of the Ocean, this great Pacific Ocean, which we [have] been so long anxious to see.* And the roaring or noise made by the waves breaking on the rocky shores (as I suppose) may be heard distinctly."

*It is now thought that what was seen from this point was the fifteen mile-wide estuary. The Pacific still lay in the distance, impossible to see from this site.

Trade Goods and Camp Equipment (Reproductions)

Missouri River traders brought an assortment of forged tools like the trammel (for pot- and meat-height adjustment over cooking fires) and "S" hooks for carrying and attaching buckets, kettles, and other sundries.

Sugar

Cone sugar was a rare treat.

The captains continued to buy dogs to eat, for the tribes on the Columbia did not want to sell us their good salmon, and the old salmon made us sick.[54] Lewis's big black dog was still with us. Its hair was matted, and it was covered with fleas. It stank. I wondered why the captains did not eat this dog. It was so big; it would have fed many. But that never happened.

Then came the day we could hear the Big Water booming . . . booming . . . booming.

Yellowheaded Blackbird

**Three Common Powder Horns
(Reproductions)**

The traders also brought firearms requiring powder, flint, and balls. These powder horns are made from animal horn and carved wood.

Clark   *December 12, 1805*

"In the evening two canoes of Clatsops visited us. . . . I can readily discover that they are close dealers and stickle for very little. [They] never close a bargain except [when] they think they have the advantage."

Clark   *December 31, 1805*

"With the party of Clatsops who visited us . . . . was a man of much lighter color than the natives are generally. He was freckled, with long dusky red hair, about 25 years of age, and must certainly be half-white at least. This man appeared to understand more of the English language than the others of his party, but did not speak a word of English. He possessed all the habits of the Indians."

"Pacific!" Lewis cried.

Here we found many tribes wearing white men's clothes and speaking white men's words.[55] There was even, among them, a tribesman who had hair of a darker red than Clark's and marks upon his face that the captains called freckles. These tribes made hard bargains for the goods we needed. I even had to trade my belt of blue beads for a robe of sea otters Lewis wanted.[56] They were better Yankee traders than the Yankee traders, Clark said.

By now, winter was closing in. The rains grew stronger. We had to build a fort in which to live until spring. But where? A vote was taken. Every man had his say, even Charbonneau. Even York, the slave man. Even me.[57] I said we should build wherever there would be enough roots to dig. But the others decided on another place.

Fire Starter Kit

The brass fire starter contained flint and steel; struck one against the other, they created a spark. To encourage the spark to flame, pre-charred fabric was carried in the fire starter. If all else failed, the magnifying glass in the fire starter's lid was used to focus the sun's rays onto tinder.

Hudson Bay Company Blanket

The stripes on the wool Hudson Bay Company blanket were referred to as "points," indicating the blanket's value. In his journals, Lewis refers to "capotes"—long, hooded coats made from these Hudson's Bay blankets—that kept his men as warm and comfortable as was possible during the wet Fort Clatsop winter.

Sheep Creek, Seven Devils Mountains, Hells Canyon Wilderness, Nez Perce National Forest, Idaho

Clark *November 24, 1805*

[Vote record re: the location of Fort Clatsop.]

"Sergt. J. Ordway   Cross and examine S.

Sergt. N. Pryor	Do	Do S. Sandy R.
Sergt. P. Gass	Do	Do S.
Jo. Shields	Proceed to Sandy R.	
Go. Shannon	Examine and cross	Falls
T.P. Howard	Do	Do Falls
P. [Weiser]	Do	Do S. R
J. Collins	Do	Do S. R
Jo. Fields	Do	Do Up
Al. Willard	Do	Do Up
R. [Windsor]	Do	Do Up
J. Potts	Do	Do Falls
R. [Frazier]	Do	Do Up
Wm. Bratton	Do	Do Up
R. Fields	Do	Do Falls
J.B. Thompson	Do	Do Up
J. Colter	Do	Do Up
H. Hall	Do	Do S. R
[LaBiche]	Do	Do S. R
Peter Cruzatte	Do	Do S. R
J.B. [LePage]	Do	Do Up
Charbonneau	—	— —
[doesn't care?]		
S. [Goodrich]	Do	Do Falls
W. Werner	Do	Do Up
Go. Gibson	Do	Do Up
Jos. Whitehouse	Do	Do Up
Geo. [Drouillard]	Examine other side	Falls
McNeal	Do	Do Up
York	Do	Do Up

Falls	Sandy River	Lookout Up
6	10	12

Janey in favor of a place where there is plenty of Potas.

[Captain Lewis] proceed on tomorrow and examine the other side. If good hunting, [we plan] to winter there, as salt is an object."

Clatsop *(KLAT-sup)*

Fort Clatsop, they called it. It was dark. It was cold. It was always wet. We were covered with fleas. It was hardship upon hardship, and want upon want. Charbonneau, Pomp, and I finally had our own sleeping place away from the others, but we suffered the same lack as everyone else. Even though many tribes visited us at the fort, we were not happy. We had very little left to trade for what we needed, and the men were growing sick on the lean elk we ate every day.

Clark's Plan for Fort Clatsop

According to Clark's drawing, the original plans for Fort Clatsop indicate a compound fifty feet square. Adjoining rooms flanked two sides, with a gate and a sentry post at either end, and a tiny parade ground at its heart. Lewis and Clark shared the captain's quarters, along with York and Seaman. The Charbonneau family had their own quarters–a first on the journey.

Bark Basket with Roots

Asked to vote on where to position Fort Clatsop, Sacagawea opted for a spot where potas were plentiful. Scholars today believe she was referring to wappato roots, commonly dug and processed in marshy areas throughout the Pacific Northwest. Wappato grows in the mud of shallow water and is harvested with the toes. Once dislodged, the egg-sized tubers float to the top of the water, are gathered by hand, then roasted, boiled, or dried. They were, and continue to be, used very much like potatoes. Also called arrowhead and tule potato, this bland, but nutritious root was a staple of the coastal peoples' diets. The word "wappato" comes from Chinook jargon.

Lewis   January 9, 1806

"The persons who usually visit the entrance of this river for the purpose of [trading] or hunting, I believe are either English or Americans. The Indians inform us that they speak the same language with ourselves, and give us proofs of their veracity by repeating many words of English: [such as] musket, powder, shot, knife, file, damned rascal, son of a bitch, etc."

Fort Clatsop (Re-creation)

Smaller than Fort Mandan, Fort Clatsop nonetheless provided some relief from the astonishingly wet winter of 1805-6. The journals note that during the entire four and a half months spent at Fort Clatsop, only twelve days were without rain; the sun appeared on a mere six of those twelve. This full-sized replica of Fort Clatsop was built in the 1950s using Clark's plan. The original fort lasted less than fifty years after the Corps' stay.

wappato *(WAH-paht-oh) (wah-PAHT-oh)*
potas *(POH-tahs)*

Ferns along Boulder Pass Trail, Glacier National Park, Montana

"At daylight this morning we were awakened by the discharge of the firearms of all our party and a salute, shouts, and a song which the whole party joined in under the windows [of the Captains' quarters]. . . . After breakfast we divided our tobacco, which amounted to 12 [twists], one half of which we gave to the men . . . who used tobacco. . . . To those who do not use it, we made a present of a handkerchief. . . . I received a present [from] Captain Lewis of fleece hosiery, shirt, drawers and socks; a pair of moccasins [from] Whitehouse; a small Indian basket [from] Goodrich; two dozen weasel tails [from] the Indian woman; and some black root [wappato or pota] from the Indians before their departure. . . . Our dinner consisted of poor elk (so spoiled that we ate it through mere necessity), some spoiled pounded fish, and a few roots."

Even on the day of Christmas, which Charbonneau said was a white man's feast day, we had only spoiled clk, spoiled fish, and a few roots to eat. Gifts of tobacco and handkerchiefs were given among the men. I gave to Clark the tails of twenty-four white weasels to ornament his clothing, as befitted a leader. But it was hard to stay happy as our stomachs rumbled.

Tobacco

Native peoples grew leaf tobacco for their own use, as well as for trade. They also blended certain plant leaves and bark to create a loose tobacco. The distinctive tobacco twists, called "pigtails" and "carrots," were the type carried by Lewis and Clark. Their shape made for easy packing and transport.

Not long after, word came that a Great Fish had washed up on the shore of the Big Water.[58] Clark and twelve of the men were going to find it, to bring back some whale meat and oil. Charbonneau told me we were to stay behind, at the fort.

I thought this very hard. Hadn't I come all this way to see the Big Water? Hadn't I endured everything the others had endured, just the same? And now there was this Monstrous Fish to be seen— and still, I would not be allowed to go?

Saltworks on the Pacific Coast (Re-enactment)

Shortly after Christmas 1805, privates William Bratton, Joseph Field, and George Gibson were ordered to establish a salt works on the Pacific coast. They built a salt cairn about fifteen miles from Fort Clatsop, near present-day Seaside, Oregon. Here they boiled ocean water, accumulating roughly twenty gallons of salt by the end of February. Some of this salt was consumed, some was used to preserve deer and elk meat, and twelve gallons were packed into ironbound kegs for use on the return journey.

Cedars and moss, Bitterroot Mountains, Clearwater National Forest, Idaho

I spoke of this to my husband in such a way, and to such an
extent, that he could no longer pretend to be deaf. So he spoke to
the captains, and finally—yes—the captains reconsidered. I would
be allowed to go.[59]

How can I tell you of this thing? Have you ever seen the Big
Water? The sky comes down, as far as the eye can see, to float upon
the face of the Lake With No Ending. The sky and the water
almost become one—far, far away.

Mountain Bluebirds

Tiger Lily, Kanisku National Forest, Idaho

Then I saw the bones of the Great Fish, anchored by the sand. Waves slapped, slapped, slapped up all around them, making foam that broke into little bundles, and piled up on the shore. All was so big and vast, I knew if I told my people what I had seen that day, they would say it could not be so. They would say it must be a Vision. Or, they would say it must be a lie.

Too soon, it was time to return to the fort. One day was the same as the next: making salt, sewing hides, making moccasins—over three hundred pair—and trying to dry out all that was dripping. Every day it rained . . . hailed . . . thundered . . . or stormed.[60] Tempers grew short. We were all anxious for spring to come so we could begin our journey home.

Granite and Moore's Lake in the distance, Gospel Hump Wilderness, Nez Perce National Forest, Idaho

Castle Peak and the Lost River Range, Challis National Forest, Idaho

Finally, it was time. Pomp was just over one year old. We left Fort Clatsop and traveled back the way we had come. Sometimes we rode in the canoes; sometimes we walked. We stopped at the camps of many tribes who remembered us.

Chief Lewis's big, black dog was captured from our camp one night, and taken toward a nearby village. Lewis was very angry and sent some of the men to rescue it. The dog was returned, but after that, extra guards were always posted.

Clark March 23, 1806

"The rain ceased and it became fair about [noon], at which time we loaded our canoes and at 1 o'clock P.M., left Fort Clatsop on our homeward-bound journey. At this place we had wintered and remained from the 7th of December, 1805 to this day. . . . [We] have lived as well as we had any right to expect, and we can say that we were never one day without three meals [per day] of some kind . . . either poor elk meat, or roots, notwithstanding the repeated fall of rain which has fallen almost constantly since we passed the long narrows . . . of November past. . . . We proceeded on."

Lewis April 11, 1806

"Three of this same tribe of villains . . . stole my dog this evening, and took him toward their village. I was shortly afterward informed of this . . . and sent three men in pursuit of the thieves with orders that, if they made the least resistance or difficulty in surrendering the dog, to fire on them. They . . . came in sight of them at the distance of about 2 miles. The Indians, discovering the party in pursuit of them, left the dog and fled."

Abalone Hair Ornaments

Abalone shell was highly prized by inland tribes for personal decoration and ceremonial use. Commonly traded by coastal tribes, the shell became more valuable each time it changed hands toward the Rocky Mountains and the plains.

Lewis   June 25, 1806

"*Last evening the Indians entertained us with setting the fir trees on fire. They have a great many number of dry limbs . . . which, when set on fire, create a very sudden and immense blaze from top to bottom of those tall trees. They are a beautiful object in this situation at night. This exhibition reminded me of a display of fireworks. . . . The natives told us that their object in setting the trees on fire was to bring fair weather for our journey. . . . At this place the squaw collected a parcel of roots of which the Shoshones eat. It is a small, knobbed root, a good deal in flavor and consistency like the Jerusalem artichoke.*"*

**This is the "Western Spring Beauty" (*Claytonia lanceolata*), according to Moulton's notes.*

At the camp of Chief Twisted Hair, we reclaimed the horses we had left with him. We dug up the caches of supplies we had buried along the way.[61] Lewis and Clark made more speeches. Dances were held in our honor. One night, young men from the tribes even set fire to the trees to bring us good weather for traveling. Like fireworks on Independence Day back in the United States, Clark told us.

Buckskin Bag With Beaded Design

Brain-tanned deer hide was widely used to make carry-all bags for both sexes. This loop strapped bag was designed to be hung from a belt, so was probably intended for a woman.

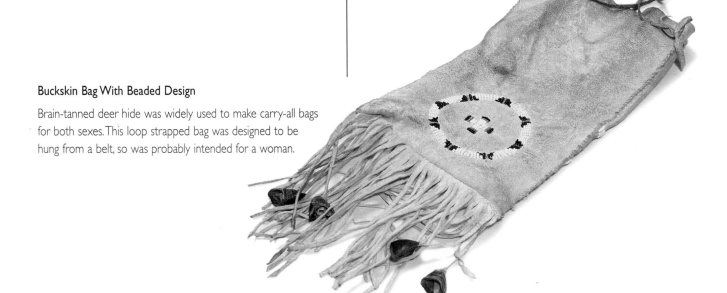

Then at the Time of the Long Grass, we broke apart.[62] Lewis took half the men and went one way. Clark and the others took fifty horses and went a different way, toward the Three Forks and the river called Yellowstone. Charbonneau, Pomp, and I went with Clark. We would meet again with Lewis on the Big River Missouri.

Lewis July 1, 1806

"From this place I determined to go with a small party by the most direct route to the Falls of the Missouri . . . to ascend Maria's River . . . to explore the country and ascertain whether any branch of that river lies as far north as latitude 50. . . . Captain Clark, with the remaining [men] including Charbonneau and York, will proceed to the Yellowstone River at its nearest approach to the Three Forks of the Missouri. Here he will build a canoe and descend the Yellowstone river with Charbonneau, the Indian woman, his servant York, and five others to the Missouri. . . . Should he arrive first, he will wait my arrival. Sergeant Pryor with two other men are to proceed [from the Three Forks] with the horses by land to the Mandans."

Clark July 3, 1806

"We collected our horses, and after breakfast I took my leave of Captain Lewis and the Indians. . . . Set out with . . . [my] men, interpreter Charbonneau and his wife and child (as interpreter and interpretress for the Crow Indians, and the latter for the Shoshone) . . . [and] fifty horses."

Nez Perce Warrior's Possessions

The traditional Nez Perce items shown here were considered "male." Each warrior had his own rawhide shield, commonly displayed on a stand when it was inside the lodge. The tubular parfleche is painted in the predominantly male colors of bright red and blue. Inside the lodge, the willow mat served as a reasonably comfortable chair back. The high-ankle moccasins are decorated with bright quillwork.

Clark   July 14, 1806

"Here the squaw informed me that there was a large road passing through the upper part of this low plain from the Madison River through the gap, which I was steering my course to . . . I saw deer, elk, . . . antelope, and a great deal of old signs of buffalo. Their roads are in every direction. . . . The Indian woman informs me that a few years ago, Buffalo were very [plentiful] in those plains and valleys, [as far as] the head of Jefferson's River, but few of them ever come into those valleys [now], owing to the Shoshones who are fearful of passing into the plains west of the mountains. [They] subsist on what game they can catch in the mountains, principally, and [on] the fish which they take in the east fork of Lewis' River. Small parties of Shoshones do pass over to the plains for a few days at a time and kill buffalo for their skin and dried meat, [but they] return immediately into the mountains."

But ours was not an easy way. The horses' feet were so sore, we had to put moccasins made of raw buffalo hide over their hooves. Wolves stole our drying meat from the scaffolds. We were chased by bears. Beaver slapped their tails all night against the water; it was impossible to sleep. And mosquitoes were so thick, the men could not see the muzzles of their guns to shoot! Pomp's face swelled to twice its size with mosquito bites, and he became very sick.

At last we came to a tall rock towering above the river. We knew it must have been a sacred place, for it was covered with markings and piles of stones. Clark climbed on top. He shouted down that behind us, he could see the Shining Mountains; in front of us, a prairie filled with buffalo, elk, and grass.

When he climbed down, he cut his name into the rock.[63] Under that, he carved the day: July 25, 1806. Then he named the place Pompey's Tower, after my Pomp.[64]

Pompey's Pillar

Named "Pompey's Tower" in 1806 in honor of Sacagawea's toddler, this sandstone monolith is now known as "Pompey's Pillar." Its shape and impact remained essentially unchanged during the hundred years between Clark's naming of it and the photographer's recording of its image.

"I proceeded on down the river on an old buffalo road. The horses' feet are very sore. Many of them can scarcely proceed on over the stone and gravel. . . . Two of the horses [are] lame, owing to their feet being worn quite smooth and to the quick. . . . I had moccasins made of [uncured] buffalo skin put on their feet, which seems to relieve them very much in passing over the stony plains."

Salmon River Pictographs

When Clark found Pompey's Tower, he noted the many pictographs and petroglyphs of the region. Generations before, the Crow Indians had painted and carved figures and symbols upon the rock of Pompey's Tower, a practice common among most native peoples. Paintings are called pictographs; carvings, petroglyphs.

William Clark's Signature at Pompey's Pillar

William Clark's 1806 signature on Pompey's Pillar is the only known physical evidence that remains on the land from the Expedition. William Clark was not the first to carve into the rock; the site was of spiritual significance to the Crow Indians—it was known by them as "The Place of the Cats" or "Where the Mountain Lion Lies"—and already bore special signs by the time Clark arrived on the scene.

Clark   July 25, 1806

"I proceeded on after the rain . . . and at 4 P.M. arrived at a remarkable rock situated in an extensive bottom[land] on the [right] side of the river and 250 paces from it. This rock, I ascended, and from its top had a most extensive view in every direction. This rock, which I shall call 'Pompey's Tower', is 200 feet high and 400 paces in circumference. . . . [It is] only accessible on one side, which is from the northeast, the other parts of it being a perpendicular cliff. . . . On top there is a tolerable soil about 5 or 6 feet thick, covered with short grass. The Indians have made two piles of stone on the top of this tower. The natives have engraved on the face of this rock the figures of animals, etc., near which I marked my name and the day of the month and year. From the top of this tower I could discover two low mountains and the Rocky Mountains covered with snow."

Immature Golden Eagle

Spittle Bug

By the Berry Moon, we met again with Lewis and the others at the Big River. Lewis was laying on his stomach in one of the boats. He had been shot, while hunting, by the fiddleman Cruzatte.

"I thought you were an elk!" Cruzatte told Lewis. But some of the men said Cruzatte had shot him on purpose.[65]

Lewis said his wounds would be better before the next moon. He wanted Clark to help him sit upright for entering the great Mandan villages.

We entered together into the place which had been our beginning. Charbonneau was paid five hundred dollars for his part in the Journey of Discovery, as had been agreed. He got not one penny extra for me. Then it was time for the captains to go. They must continue downriver until they reached the Great Father.

Clark wanted to take Pomp with him to live in his house, to teach him white men's ways, to be his son. I knew Clark felt affection for Pomp. But how could I let him go? My dancing boy had barely found his legs. He was not even weaned. No! Pomp would stay with me!

Mandan Earth Lodge, Lewis and Clark Trail, West Bank, Missouri

Though this earth lodge was most likely photographed in the early 1900s, it is virtually identical to those built two hundred years before. Warm in winter, cool in summer, earth lodges were of very sound ecological design.

Clark August 12, 1806

"At [noon] Captain Lewis hove into sight. . . . I was alarmed, on the landing of the canoes, to be informed that Captain Lewis was wounded by an accident. I found him lying in the pirogue. He informed me that his wound was slight and he would be well in 20 or 30 days. . . . I examined the wound and found it a very bad flesh wound. The ball had passed through the fleshy part of his left thigh below the hipbone, and cut the cheek of the right buttock for three inches in length [at] the depth of the ball. . . . Captain Lewis informed me that the accident happened the day before [when] one of the men, Peter Cruzatte, [mistook] him in the thick bushes to be an elk [and shot him]. . . . Captain Lewis, thinking it Indians who had shot him, hobbled to the canoes as fast as possible and was followed by Cruzatte. The mistake was then discovered."

"I was about to shake [hands] with the Grand Chiefs of all the villages there assembled. They requested me to sit one minute longer with them, which I readily agreed to, and directed a pipe to be lit. The Chiefs informed me that when we first came to their country, they did not believe all we then told to them. But they were now convinced that everything we had told them [was] true, that they should keep in memory everything which we had said to them, and strictly attend to our advice. . . . We then saluted them with a gun, and set out [for St. Louis]."

But then Charbonneau said, "Yes. When the boy is older." And the men clasped their hands in agreement.[66]

I stood on the bank of the river, holding onto Pomp. Lewis and Clark's canoes were going one way–white trappers' and traders' canoes were going the other. Yet I knew they were all going to the same place: to the Land of Tomorrow.

This was the end of my journey; this was the beginning of a Great Change. I understood that what I had seen–the lands I had passed through, the lands of my people and others like them–would never again be the same.[67]

I tell you these things that they may be remembered with truth and respect. Ah-hi-e! It is good that you remember.

Turkey Feather Fan

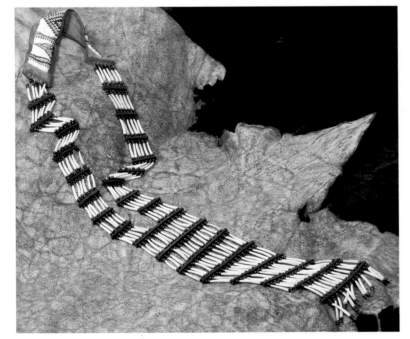

Dentalium Shell Necklace

This valuable necklace has dentalium shells interspersed with blue beads, then connected with a beaded neckstrap. Dentalium was a highly prized shell, traded inward from the Pacific Northwest coast, and used both as decoration and money.

Beargrass, Nez Perce National Forest, Idaho

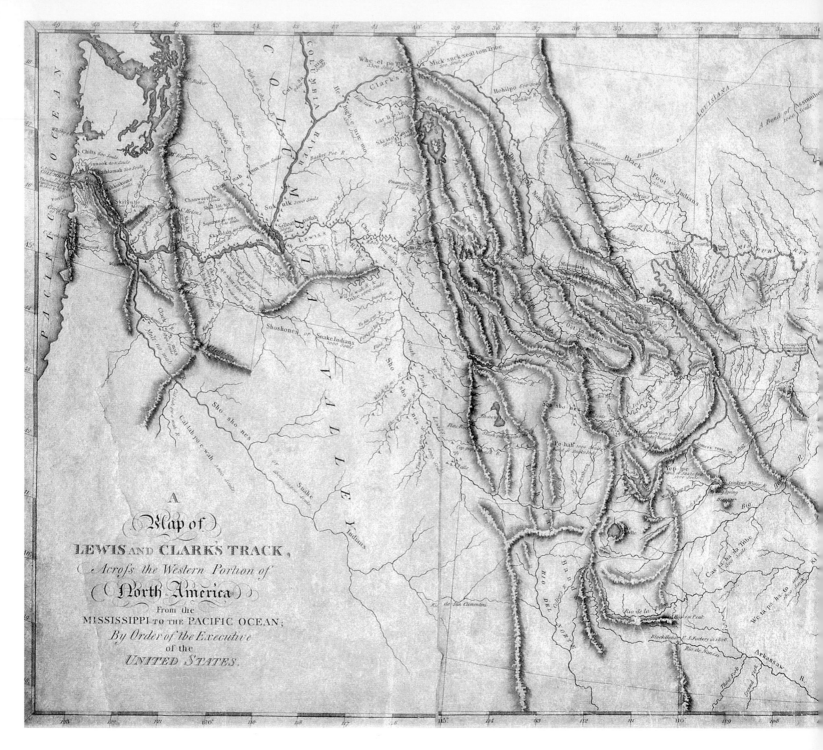

Clark   Letter to Charbonneau (excerpt)
written en route to St. Louis
August 20, 1806

". . . Your woman, who accompanied you that long, dangerous, and fatiguing route to the Pacific Ocean and back, deserved a greater reward for her attention and services on that route than we had in our power to give her."

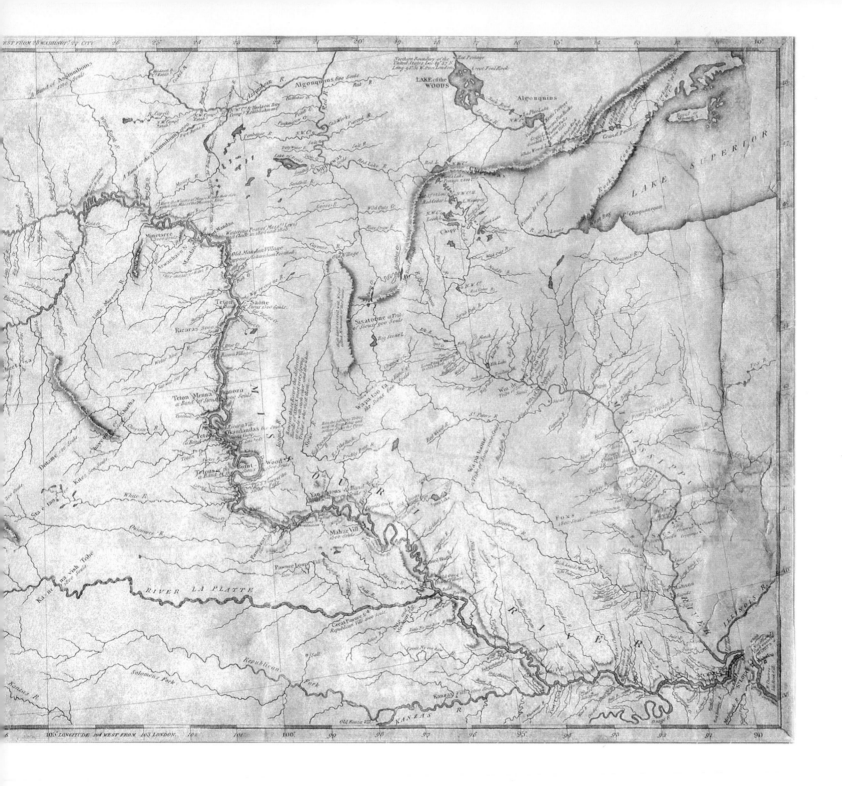

Timeline

1738   French fur trader Pierre de la Vérendrye arrives among the Knife River Mandans of the upper Missouri River, the first non-native known to make contact here.

1776   The signing of the Declaration of Independence marks the beginning of the American Revolution.

1784   The North West Company is established in Montreal, Canada, to challenge the Hudson's Bay Company's control of the fur trade on the Northern Plains.

1787   The US Northwest Ordinance sets guidelines for settlement of the American frontier, including prohibition of slavery, and a requirement to deal fairly with the Indians.

1788   The ship *Columbia*, captained by Robert Gray of Boston, gives its name to the river it explores on the Pacific Northwest coast, thereby establishing US claims to the region. Gray trades iron tools, mirrors, and trinkets for otter furs with the Northwest Indians.

1789   Sacagawea is born (?). The exact date is unknown. It is generally agreed within the academic community that Sacagawea was about sixteen years old when she was on the Expedition, which would put her birth around 1789.

         George Washington is inaugurated as first president of the United States.

1793   North West Company fur trader Alexander MacKenzie becomes the first non-native known to cross the North American continent. From his trading post on Lake Athabasca in what is now Alberta, Canada, MacKenzie crosses the Rocky Mountains and travels through British Columbia, eventually canoeing down the Bella Coola River to the Pacific Ocean. He publishes a book about his travels.

1799	Sacagawea is taken captive by the Minnetaree at Three Forks (?). Oral tradition holds that Sacagawea was ten or eleven years old at the time of her capture.

George Washington dies.

1800	The US capital is moved from Philadelphia to Washington.

1801	Thomas Jefferson is inaugurated as third president of the United States.

Meriwether Lewis becomes Jefferson's personal secretary and begins the studies that will prepare him for the Corps of Discovery Expedition.

1803	The United States buys the Louisiana Purchase from France for $15,000,000, effectively doubling the size of the country.

Jefferson asks Congress for $2,500 for an expedition to find the Northwest Passage. (Modern historians estimate the total cost for the Expedition—in 1806-dollars—came to $38,000.)

William Clark accepts Lewis's invitation to join the Expedition.

Sacagawea becomes the wife of Toussaint Charbonneau. (Approximate date.)

1804	Napoleon crowns himself emperor of France.

The Corps of Discovery departs from its headquarters near St. Louis, and heads toward the Mandan villages on the Knife River. Here, the men construct Fort Mandan, where they will spend the winter.

1804	Charbonneau offers his services to Lewis and Clark as an interpreter. He says he has wives of the Snake (Shoshone) tribe, whose homelands the Corps must cross. He says the Shoshones have horses on which to cross the Shining Mountains.

1805   Sacagawea's son Pomp is born, February 11.

Lewis and Clark's Corps of Discovery departs the Mandan villages for The Great Unknown. The same day, a shipment of specimens and reports pushes off in the opposite direction for St. Louis, and ultimately, President Jefferson. The date is April 7.

Lewis reaches the Great Falls of the Missouri River, June 13.

Sacagawea is reunited with her birth people, the Agui Dika, August 17. She adopts Bazil, her sister's orphaned son.

The Corps of Discovery reaches the Pacific Ocean, November 18.

Sacagawea's belt of blue beads is traded by Lewis and Clark for a robe of sea otter skins, November 20.

Sacagawea, Charbonneau, and York are asked to vote with the rest of the Corps as to where winter quarters should be built, November 24.

Fort Clatsop is completed. On the Expedition, Sacagawea, Charbonneau, and Pomp are given their own personal quarters for the first time. The date is December 30.

1806   Sacagawea sees the Pacific Ocean and The Big Fish for the first time, January 8.

The Corps of Discovery begins its return trip, March 23.

The Expedition divides on June 29. Lewis and his party go north to explore the Marias River country. Clark and his party take fifty horses, Sacagawea, Charbonneau, Pomp, and York past the Three Forks to the Yellowstone River.

1806   Clark names Pompey's Tower after Sacagawea's son, July 25.

The Corps of Discovery is reunited at the Missouri River. They enter the Mandan villages they had left a year and four months prior. Charbonneau is paid five hundred dollars for his services as an interpreter on the Expedition. Sacagawea is paid nothing. Lewis, Clark, and the rest of the Corps say their farewells, and head downriver for civilization. The date is August 17, one year to the day after Sacagawea was reunited with her Shoshoni relatives, and was able to secure horses on which the Corps could cross the Shining Mountains.

Clark writes Charbonneau a letter expressing his gratitude for the services of both Charbonneau and Sacagawea on the Expedition. He restates his desire to take Pomp with him, to educate and raise him "as my own child." Clark's offer has no time limit, but he encourages Charbonneau to bring "my little dancing boy, Baptiste," as soon as he possibly can. The date is August 20.

Lewis and Clark return to St. Louis, September 23. Just outside of town, they pass Daniel Boone's home, where the American frontier legend still lives. Lewis and Clark have been gone so long without any word, most people assume they are long dead. There is a great banquet and welcoming ball in their honor.

Lewis begins writing his report to President Jefferson, September 26. Jefferson later nominates Lewis to be Governor of the Territory of Louisiana.

1808   Clark becomes a partner in the Missouri Fur Company, which plans to send militia, hunters, and boatmen up the Missouri to develop the American fur trade.

1809   Lewis dies on the Natchez Trace while traveling to Washington, DC. Most modern scholars agree he killed himself.

Abraham Lincoln is born in Kentucky.

1810	Sacagawea and Charbonneau arrive in St. Louis, where they entrust Pomp, Pomp's sister Lizette, and his half brother Toussaint into the care of William Clark.
1811	The Pacific Fur Company, founded by John Jacob Astor, establishes Fort Astoria at the mouth of the Columbia River. The site is not far from that of Fort Clatsop, where Sacagawea spent the winter five years earlier.
1812	"This evening the wife of Charbonneau, a Snake squaw, died of a putrid fever. She was a good [woman] and the best woman in the fort. Aged about 25 years. She left a fine infant girl." —Factor Luttig, Fort Manuel, SD. December 20, 1812.
1813	Clark is appointed Governor of the Missouri Territory and Superintendent of Indian Affairs. He files for official guardianship of Sacagawea's children Pomp and Lizette, and Charbonneau's son, Toussaint (Jr.).
1816	York is finally granted his freedom. The exact date is in question, but it was at least a decade after the Expedition.
1823	Pomp becomes a favorite of Prince Paul Wilhelm of Wuertemberg, Germany, who meets Pomp in a trader's village at the mouth of the Kansas River. Pomp accompanies Prince Paul Wilhelm to Europe, where he lives at court for six years before returning to the Western frontier.
1833	Artist George Catlin visits the Knife River villages and paints many scenes of everyday life, thus providing the first popular view of life as Sacagawea would have known it.
1834	Artist Karl Bodmer visits the Knife River villages with Maximilian, Prince of Wied-Neuwied, to paint scenes from the prince's expedition. One of their guides is Sacagawea's husband Toussaint Charbonneau.
1837	A smallpox epidemic nearly eliminates the Mandans and Minnetaree.

1838	William Clark dies.
1842	Toussaint Charbonneau, Sacagawea's husband, dies. (Approximate date.)
1843	The first mass migration over the Oregon Trail begins.
1849	Gold discovered in California gives rise to the Gold Rush.
1860	Abraham Lincoln is elected sixteenth president of the United States.
1861–65	The United States fights the Civil War.
1884	"The burial of Sacajawea took place late in the afternoon of the day on which she died [April 9]. Those in attendance were her immediate family, the Indian Agent, and some of the [reservation] employees. I read, over her grave, the Burial Service of the Episcopal Church."

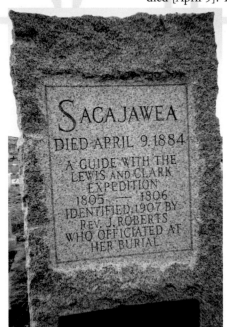

The inscription on the gravestone reads: "Sacajawea Died April 9th, 1884. A guide with Lewis and Clark Expedition. Identified by Rev. John Roberts, Who Officiated At Her Burial."

—Rev. John Roberts, 1884.
Wind River Indian Reservation,
Fort Washakie, Wyoming.

Expedition Supply List

On June 17, 1803, Captain Lewis listed articles purchased for the Expedition in general groups such as camp equipment and materials, mathematical instruments, medicines, gifts for the Indians, provisions, transportation, and weaponry.

Listed under "Camp Equipage" are such items as tents, oiled packing bags, tin horns, lamps, square plates, cups without handles (because they were easier to pack), knives, spoons, and a corn grinding mill. Also listed are fishing hooks, brass kettles, gold scales and weights, large shears, needles and awls, rasps, files, vices, pliers, saws, chisels, adzes, augers, hatchets, and a whet stone. Add to this eight receipt books, six brass inkwells, half a dozen envelopes of ink powder, one hundred writing quills, and a pound of sealing wax for securing documents and letters. Raw materials for camp included tent canvas, linen and sheeting, oiling (waterproofing), thread and cording, hooks and eyes.

Mathematical instruments secured for the trip included a level, platting and surveying instruments, several pocket compasses plus a brass boat compass, a magnet, sextant, microscope and "slates," and four ounces of talc. Also listed were a circular protractor and index, a six-inch pocket telescope, nautical tables and charts, a "parallel glass for the horizon," and a chronometer with keys to allow for extremely accurate readings of time when calculating position. In addition, several scientific guides on the subjects of mineralogy, botany, and "spherics" were purchased.

Gifts for the Indians included such items as pipe tomahawks, red flannel, silk ribbon, scarlet cloth, striped India silk, calico ruffled shirts, needles, thimbles, knitting pins, scissors, and sewing awls. Add, of course, beads of various descriptions, pocket looking glasses, iron combs, small "jingle" bells, pewter buttons, earrings, lockets, brooches, and (truly indispensable) 432 curtain rings! More brass kettles are listed, as are sheet iron, two corn grinders, fish hooks, knives (butcher knives and others), blankets, red lead and vermillion, plus 130 pigtail twists of tobacco. And, finally, a trunk in which to pack it all.

The "provisions" category of Lewis's list began with 193 pounds of portable soup and 30 gallons of wine in 6 kegs. This was followed by flannel shirts, a variety of coats, blankets, overalls, "frocks" (uniforms?), shirts, shoes, and stockings.

Under "arms and accoutrements," Lewis listed a pair of pocket pistols, a pair of "horseman's pistols," muskets, powder horns and pouches, 500 rifle flints, gun slings, and brushes and wires for cleaning the arms. In addition, 420 pounds of sheet lead were packed for making balls, and 2 separate orders of gunpowder: 176 pounds of general gunpowder, and 50 pounds of the "best rifle powder." The powder was to be stored in 52 lead canisters. Fifteen painted knapsacks joined 15 "cartouch boxes" (named for the shape), and assorted "scalping knives" and knife belts.

We know from other records that by the time the Corps of Discovery embarked on its journey, the men had not only muskets, but also rifles, espontoons (spear-headed braces against which rifles could be steadied, and which could be also be used alone as weapons), bayonets, and swords. They also had an air gun (a rarity for the time), a swivel cannon, and a pair of blunderbusses that were mounted on the keelboat.

Lewis's list concludes with "1 boat and her caparison [equipment], including spiked poles, boat-hooks, and tow line." A separate notation tells us that several securing and towing lines of varying materials were purchased, along with 70 large hooks and one "Sportsman's flask." Missing was any mention of Lewis's ingenious (but doomed) collapsible boat *The Experiment*.

What did Captain Lewis estimate the cost of all this to be? He suggested a figure of about $2,500 in the currency of the day, the amount Jefferson requested from Congress for the Expedition. According to Lewis and Clark historian Michael Carrick, however, the full cost came to over ten and one-half times that amount. In terms of 1806-dollars, the final cost of the Expedition was close to $38,000.

Espontoon
(Spear-headed braces against which rifles could be steadied)

This *espontoon* dates to circa 1800, and was bought at auction from a Smithsonian Museum deaccession. *Espontoons* were carried by infantry officers through the eighteenth century, often instead of muskets. *Espontoons* could be used to brace rifles and muskets for more accurate shooting, or could be used alone as weapons. Lewis and Clark record killing snakes and wolves with their *espontoons*, fending off a brown bear on the prod, and using the *espontoon* shaft to keep their balance in areas of unsure footing.

Kentucky Rifle

This Kentucky rifle was made about 1790 by Jacob Christ in Frederick, Maryland. It is known that Captain Clark and Drouillard (Drewyer) had hunting rifles, probably very similar to this one. Clark's journal entry of December 10, 1805, states that his small rifle used balls of a size 100 to the pound–roughly .38 caliber. The Harper's Ferry rifles were .54 caliber, and the muskets were .69 caliber. In referring to his "small" rifle, Clark was actually referring to the "small" caliber.

Pocket Pistols

The size and style of these pocket pistols would have been familiar to both Lewis and Clark. One pair with "secret triggers" was purchased for ten dollars by Captain Lewis on May 23, 1803 from one Robert Barnhill. On April 29, 1806, Clark's journal states that one of Lewis's pistols, plus several hundred rounds of ammunition, were traded for "a fine horse." Clark, himself, had made such a trade while among Sacagawea's people the previous summer: one pistol, one hundred balls with powder, and a knife–all traded for one horse.

US Model 1803 Harper's Ferry Rifle

Though this model is commonly called the "Lewis and Clark Expedition Rifle," it did not go into production until almost a year after Lewis left Harper's Ferry Arsenal with fifteen "half stocked short rifles." Scholars think the rifles commissioned by Lewis were precursors of this model.

Swivel Blunderbuss

Made circa 1800, this flintlock swivel gun is probably similar to two of the three guns mounted on the bow and stern of the Expedition keelboat for its trip up the Missouri River. They are called "swivels," and occasionally, "cannon," in the journals. It is thought there was one swivel-mounted, traditional cannon on the bow of the keelboat, and two swivel blunderbusses on the stern. Sergeant Ordway notes in his journal on September 25, 1804, that the swivel cannon was loaded with sixteen musket balls; the two smaller blunderbusses, with buckshot. These two smaller "cannon" were stored in a cache near Great Falls, Montana, for retrieval on the return journey.

Swivel Cannon

This is the style of small cannon that was mounted on the bow of the Expedition keel boat. According to the journals, it was used not only for protection and intimidation, but was also fired at sunrise, July 4, 1804, to honor the day. Upon the Expedition's successful return to the Mandan villages in August 1806, it was decided to make a present of the "swivel gun" to One Eye, the Great Chief of the Minnetaree. Clark's stated purpose was to "ingratiate him more strongly in our favor," whereupon the cannon was conveyed immediately to One Eye's village.

Pipe Tomahawk

This is an original pipe tomahawk from the era spanning 1790 through 1820. The unusual amount of silver inlay on this tomahawk (nineteen pieces) may indicate that it was a piece of importance, possibly a presentation piece to a chief. The Expedition supply list shows twelve pipe tomahawks purchased to be given as "Indian presents." On June 2, 1806, Clark praises Drouillard for retrieving a stolen tomahawk which "we prized most as it was the private property of the late Sergeant Floyd, and I was desirous of returning it to his friends."

Spontoon-type Tomahawk

This is a replica of a type of tomahawk shaped somewhat like a *spontoon*. It is conceivable that the first tomahawks of this type actually were fashioned from broken *spontoons*. Lewis observes that the Expedition blacksmiths were kept busy fabricating tomahawk blades for the residents of the Mandan and Minnetaree villages. His journal entry for February 5, 1805, is accompanied by a sketch of this type of tomahawk.

Tomahawk—Missouri War Axe

This is an original tomahawk head. It is the same type Lewis and Clark found, already in use, along the Missouri River. The Expedition blacksmiths turned out many of these on their forges during the long winter at Fort Mandan. Though Lewis thought it of poor design, the "Missouri War Axe" was most popular. It weighed about one pound total—a convenient weight—but, in Lewis's opinion, the great length of the blade topping the smallish handle "render[ed] a stroke uncertain and easily avoided." He also thought the short handle rendered too shallow a blow to do much damage, particularly from horseback.

Air Gun

This air gun is of the period from 1800 through 1820. Until recent years, scholars thought the air rifle (cited repeatedly in Lewis's journals) was the type with an attached, hollow, ball-shaped "air chamber." Now, however, it is generally agreed that the air gun Lewis used had a "butt reservoir" like this one. The rifle was primed or charged by pumping air into the reservoir located in the butt end—somewhere between five hundred to seven hundred strokes for a full charge! The gun shown here is of European origin. Lewis's gun was made in Philadelphia. It would have been operated in the same way, but would have looked more like a full-stocked American flintlock rifle of the period.

Corps of Discovery
Leaving Fort Mandan For The Pacific

Lewis's journal entry of April 7, 1805, lists the following individuals
(given here alphabetically) as accompanying him and Captain Clark:

Sergeants	Privates	Interpreters
Patrick Gass	William Bratton	Toussaint Charbonneau
John Ordway	John Collins	George Drouillard (Drewyer)
Nathaniel Pryor	John Colter	
	Peter (Pierre) Cruzatte	
	Joseph Fields	
	Reuben Fields	
	Robert Frazier	
	George Gibson	
	Silas Goodrich	
	Hugh Hall	
	Thomas P. Howard	
	Francis (François) Labiche (LaBiche)	
	John Baptiste Lepage (LePage)	
	Hugh McNeal	
	John Potts	
	George Shannon	
	John Shields	
	John B. Thompson	
	William Werner	
	Joseph Whitehouse	
	Alexander Willard	
	Richard Windsor	
	Peter Weiser (Wiser)	

Lewis lists: "also a black man by the name of York, servant to Captain Clark; an Indian woman, wife to Charbonneau, with a young child; and a Mandan man who had promised . . . to accompany us as far as the Snake Indians, with a view to bring about a good understanding . . . between that nation and his own. . . ."

It was not uncommon for the Corps to be joined at various times during their journey by different tribesmen and women, who accompanied them as guides, advisors, or simply companions over certain portions of the route. Missing from the Corps of Discovery by this time were three of the original members: John Newman, sent back for "mutinous expression"; Moses Reed, dismissed for desertion; and Charles Floyd, who had died of "bilious colic" (possibly a ruptured appendix) before ever reaching the Mandan villages. Sergeant Floyd was the only fatality suffered by the Corps during their entire trip.

It had been planned all along that some of the original Corps would return to St. Louis when the others left Fort Mandan for the Pacific. The former group would take back letters, specimens, and articles of scientific interest to "the U States" and President Jefferson.

Newman and Reed, in their disgrace, joined Corporal Richard Warfington's return party of four additional soldiers and four hired boatmen. The date was April 7, 1805, the same day the rest of the Expedition launched itself west toward the Shining Mountains.

Sacagawea

It is thought that the woman we call Sacagawea was born among the Lemhi Shoshones about 1789, the same year George Washington was inaugurated first president of the United States. Ten or eleven years later, she was captured by the Minnetaree (Hidatsa) from the Three Forks region of present-day Montana. Sacagawea's band was in one of its traditional summer hunting camps when the raiding Minnetaree struck, taking Sacagawea and other young girls captive. For the next five or so years, she lived among the Minnetaree in the confederated Hidatsa/Mandan villages situated along the Missouri at its juncture with the Knife River (in present-day North Dakota). She was most likely adopted into a Minnetaree clan during her time there, as this was the usual procedure among her captors. The belt of blue beads Sacagawea was known to have worn was an indication that, not only had she been "made a relative" among the Minnetaree, but she was also highly regarded as a hard worker.

Exactly how Sacagawea became the woman—or wife—of French-Canadian trapper/trader Toussaint Charbonneau, is not known. Charbonneau may have purchased Sacagawea outright, or won her as the result of a bet or gamble. It is known that she became Charbonneau's mate about a year before Lewis and Clark came to the Mandan villages in the winter of 1804-5. She joined another of Charbonneau's Shoshoni wives, and his son, in the Second Village. It was not unusual for a man to have more than one wife among the Minnetaree and the Mandan, as long as he could provide for and protect them. Among the traders and trappers, it was even more common.

When Lewis and Clark arrived in the Mandan villages, Sacagawea was already pregnant. She gave birth to Jean Baptiste Charbonneau (more commonly known as Pomp, which means "first-born" in the Shoshoni language) on February 11, 1805. Not quite two months later, the Corps of Discovery left the Mandan villages to find a river route from the Missouri to the Pacific Ocean. Toussaint Charbonneau and Sacagawea (with Pomp) accompanied them as interpreters. Charbonneau spoke both French and Hidatsa; Sacagawea spoke Hidatsa and Shoshoni. Between them, they would provide a crucial language link in Lewis and Clark's negotiations for Shoshoni horses. In addition, Sacagawea's presence among this

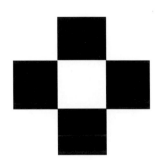

party of thirty-three military men—particularly carrying her infant, Pomp—immediately signaled to native peoples that the group's intent was peaceful.

Along the route, Sacagawea dug up edible roots, picked berries, and collected wild plants to use as food or medicine. Undoubtedly, she helped dress hides, made and repaired moccasins and clothing, and continued to carry out the same "women's tasks" that would have been her duty back in the Second Village. Lewis and Clark's journals do not seem to indicate, however, whether Sacagawea was expected to cook while on the journey; this would have been a big change for her. There is mention made that she broke animal bones and drained the marrow from them but, otherwise, the camp cooking duties fell to the men, including Charbonneau.

When the Corps of Discovery did meet with Sacagawea's people—the "Salmon Eaters" or Lemhi Shoshones—Sacagawea's skill as an interpreter successfully secured horses on which the Corps could cross the Shining Mountains. This was vital. Without horses, the Corps would not have been able to make its way to the Columbia River and, from there, to the Pacific Ocean. Without horses, the Corps would most probably have starved to death in the mountains.

It was a tremendous surprise to all involved that Cameahwait, Sacagawea's clan brother, had become the leader of this Shoshoni band in Sacagawea's absence. In a scene right out of Hollywood, their unexpected reunion tugged at the heartstrings of those watching, and further cemented the relationship between the Shoshones and the Corps of Discovery. One of Sacagawea's childhood friends, who had been captured by the Minnetarees with Sacagawea but had escaped, was also found to be living among the Salmon Eaters when the Corps came into camp. Lewis recorded in his journal that their discovery of one another was "really affecting . . .".

As the Expedition moved through Sacagawea's Shoshoni homeland, she remembered trails and passes that would ease and shorten the Corps' journey. In this sense, she did help guide Lewis and Clark through this portion of the journey. However, her primary function was that of interpreter.

During the long winter spent on the Pacific coast, Sacagawea was asked to vote for a location upon which to build winter quarters. Her practical opinion, as stated in the journals, called for a fort to be built wherever there would be enough roots to eat. The men had other

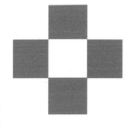

ideas and she was outvoted, but historians consider this the first official US vote by a woman. Though native women (particularly in east coast tribes) had long been given leadership roles and were entitled to official vote, apparently this occasion marked the first time a woman was asked to vote in a "sovereign U.S." situation. Because generations would pass before women were given the constitutional right to vote, Sacagawea's action in 1805 is an important milestone in American history.

During that long winter, Sacagawea's treasured belt of blue beads was traded in exchange for a robe of sea otter skins that Lewis wanted. It is recorded that the captains tried to effect the exchange with all manner of trade goods, but the native traders specifically wanted the "chief beads" of blue that were available only in Sacagawea's belt. The journals do not remark on what Sacagawea thought of this particular trade, but apparently she held no grudge. In fact, she gave Captain Clark two dozen weasel tails as a Christmas gift so that he could ornament his new clothing. Where Sacagawea obtained the tails—whether she had killed the animals herself, traded for them, or received them as a gift—is not clear. Nor is there any reference to gifts she may have received in return for her generosity.

On the return leg of the Expedition in the summer of 1806, Lewis and Clark divided forces. Lewis took some of the men north (into present-day Montana) to explore the upper regions of the Marias River. Clark took the rest of the men, fifty horses, Charbonneau, Sacagawea, and Pomp down the Yellowstone River. It was here that Clark dedicated Pompey's Tower in honor of Sacagawea's "dancing boy," Jean Baptiste (Pomp). The site's name has since been changed to Pompey's Pillar.

When the Corps returned to the Mandan villages in August 1806, Charbonneau was paid for his participation in the expedition. He was also given a grant of 320 acres of land, should he decide to farm, and letters of recommendation from Captain Clark for his service. Sacagawea was given nothing. In a letter written to Charbonneau after the Corps had left the Mandan villages, Clark praises Sacagawea's contributions to the Expedition and expresses regret that the Corps did not have it in their power to reward her.

Clark had become quite fond of Pomp during the journey. He asked to take Pomp with him when he left the Mandan villages; he promised to raise Pomp as his own son, teach him white men's ways, and pay for Pomp's schooling. Clark's notes on the event say that both Charbonneau and Sacagawea were willing to have him do this, but that Pomp was not yet weaned so the arrangement was postponed. There is no direct record from Sacagawea as to what she thought of the proposal at the time.

It is thought that in late 1809, she accompanied Charbonneau to St. Louis to deliver Pomp to Clark. Documentation proves that, almost a decade after the expedition, Clark did file for legal guardianship of not only Pomp, but also Lizette Charbonneau and Toussaint Charbonneau (Jr.). The most commonly held view is that Lizette was the daughter of Sacagawea; Toussaint (Jr.) was the son of Charbonneau and his other Shoshoni wife at the Second Village.

Six years after the Expedition, on December 20, 1812, Charbonneau was at Fort Manuel in present-day South Dakota. Fort Manuel was a Missouri Fur Company trading post at the time. He was accompanied by a Shoshoni, or "Snake," wife. Factor Luttig of the fort states that this "wife of Charbonneau, a Snake squaw, died of a putrid fever" during the night, and that she left an infant girl as survivor. Many historians are convinced that this Shoshoni wife of Charbonneau was, indeed, Sacagawea, citing Clark's "Se-car-ja-we-au . . . Dead" notation in his journals of 1825-8, and emphasizing the fact that Clark adopted Pomp, Lizette, and Toussaint (Jr.) less than a year after the 1812 date.

There is, however, strong oral tradition among Sacagawea's people that she lived a long and interesting life after the Expedition, and that she died in 1884 at approximately one hundred years of age on the Wind River Indian Reservation in present-day Wyoming. These traditions say she eventually left Charbonneau and traveled widely among her relatives, even speaking in council with the revered Chief Washakie. Her adopted son Bazil (or Shoogan) is buried beside her on the Reservation. A granite marker dedicated to Pomp stands there also.

Where did Sacagawea die? Where is she buried? Only you can decide what to believe.

Toussaint Charbonneau

Born around 1759, Toussaint Charbonneau was approximately forty-four years old when he became the husband of fourteen-year-old Sacagawea. A French-Canadian/mixed-blood by birth, Charbonneau had become a trader/trapper in his adulthood and, for a time, worked for the North West Company. By the time Lewis and Clark made his acquaintance, Charbonneau had lived among the tribes for about ten years, the last five of which had been spent among the Minnetaree (Hidatsa) on the upper Missouri. It is known he already had at least one Shoshoni wife when Sacagawea came into his life. He also had a son named Toussaint who lived with him.

When Lewis and Clark came to the Mandan villages, they were looking to hire interpreters for their journey to the Pacific Ocean. They wanted men with a knowledge of, not only the land they were to navigate, but also the customs and languages of the native peoples whose homelands they were to cross. Charbonneau fit this criteria. He spoke both French and Minnetaree (Hidatsa). When Lewis and Clark learned that he had wives who spoke Shoshoni and who could help the Corps secure horses for their arduous trek across the Rocky Mountains, Charbonneau became a prime candidate for hire. Apparently, Charbonneau recognized his value for he tried to up the ante; he refused to take orders and made demands that abruptly put him out of consideration. Discovering the predicament his self-importance had created, however, he quickly agreed to the captains' terms and became one of the permanent party.

Lewis and Clark traveled with Charbonneau, Sacagawea, and the infant Jean Baptiste (Pomp) for one year and four months. During this time, the journals indicate that Charbonneau was probably typical of trader/trappers of his time. The entry describing him to be "of no particular merit" seems harsh, given that his language skills were vital in the negotiations for horses. We do know that Charbonneau was prone to panic, that he got into trouble easily, that he chafed under discipline, and that he struck his wife when irritated with her. These traits were not unique to Charbonneau. With the exception of the panic attacks he suffered, especially on the rivers, the traits ascribed to Charbonneau in the journals could be used to describe most trader/trappers or "mountain men" of that–and subsequent–eras.

We know he cooked an outstanding *boudin blanc* (white pudding) which became a favorite of Lewis. This delicacy was made by stuffing buffalo intestines with raw meat, organ meats, hard fat, flour, and salt, then boiling it until almost cooked through. Finally, this sausage was fried in grease or fat (usually bear) until browned. When the Corps was in buffalo country, Lewis appointed Charbonneau "camp cook" as often as possible so the French-Canadian could make these white puddings regularly.

A situation–with potentially drastic consequences for Charbonneau–arose when the Corps was in Sacagawea's home village among the Shoshones. In accordance with Shoshoni tradition, Sacagawea's father had promised his daughter in marriage to a tribesman when

Sacagawea was still a child. Now that she was reunited with her people as an adult, the prospective bridegroom appeared in council, claiming his right to her as his wife. He already had two wives in camp, but it was his right to claim Sacagawea. The journals say he finally relented when he discovered she had an infant by another husband. There is no record of Charbonneau's reaction.

The rest of Charbonneau's service with the Corps is without extraordinary incident. He hunted; he explored; he translated; he interpreted. In August 1806, when the Corps returned to the Mandan villages on the Missouri River, Charbonneau was paid $500.33 for his service, plus a grant of 320 acres of land. He and Sacagawea returned to their normal lives at the Second Village. Most probably they were reunited with Charbonneau's other Shoshoni wife and son Toussaint. For three years, Charbonneau disappears from the record books. Then, in late 1809, we learn that Charbonneau traveled to St. Louis where he sold his land grant voucher back to Clark for one hundred dollars. It is thought Sacagawea accompanied him. Pomp was left with Clark to begin his schooling. Oral tradition maintains that Toussaint (Jr.) was also left with Clark at this time.

Charbonneau then signed on with the Missouri Fur Company. Charbonneau himself continued to live among the Minnetaree at the Second Village. He carried out some diplomatic duties on the upper Missouri during the War of 1812, and was imprisoned for a short time by the Spanish while on an expedition to Santa Fe in 1815. As Superintendent of Indian Affairs, Clark continued to employ Charbonneau, in the region of the upper Missouri, as a government interpreter for visiting dignitaries, government officials, explorers and artists. Charbonneau likely would have known George Catlin in the Mandan villages when the artist was producing his sketches and paintings. Charbonneau also acted as guide for the party in which Karl Bodmer created his famous works.

Charbonneau finally disappeared from government service rolls the year after William Clark died, following a trip he made to St. Louis to collect back pay. In his mid-seventies, he was apparently still wooing the ladies. Letters have been found from that time period, saying that Charbonneau "is always marrying someone."

His estate was settled in 1843 by his son Jean Baptiste Charbonneau.

Jean Baptiste Charbonneau (Pomp)

This first-born son of Sacagawea and her husband Toussaint Charbonneau led an extraordinary life. Born February 11, 1805, inside Fort Mandan on the Missouri River, this infant was named after his paternal grandfather. His Shoshoni name, however, was Pomp, which meant "first born" in Sacagawea's birth language. He joined at least one other Charbonneau brother, Toussaint (Jr.), who lived in the Minnetaree village with his Shoshoni mother, another wife of Toussaint Charbonneau.

Pomp was only fifty-five days old when the Corps of Discovery set out from the Mandan Villages on its expedition to the Pacific Ocean. It is probable he rode much of the journey in a cradleboard, or sling, on his mother's back. The cradleboard was lost in a flash flood in the vicinity of the Great Falls of the Missouri during the summer. It is not known whether Sacagawea made another.

When Pomp's mother was reunited with her birth people that August of 1805, she formally adopted the orphaned son of her dead sister. In this way, Pomp acquired a brother named Bazil (Shoogan), and Sacagawea, a second son. Instead of being Bazil's aunt, Sacagawea was, in accordance with tribal custom, now considered his mother. Because the Journals do not mention him after this, it is assumed that Bazil stayed with the Lemhi Shoshones instead of accompanying his new mother to the Pacific Ocean.

From the journals, we know that Pomp grew very sick on the return journey of 1806. He had a high fever and swollen face, neck, and throat. It is not known whether he was teething, had mumps or tonsillitis, or whether he had contracted an infection. What is known is that Sacagawea placed warm poultices of wild onions on his neck, followed by a salve made from pine resin, beeswax, and bear oil. This concoction was bandaged over to form a "plaster." In two and a half weeks, Pomp was better.

He also fell prey to the clouds of mosquitoes that plagued the Corps on the Yellowstone River. His face swelled up grotesquely from their bites. He was, no doubt, miserable. A common mosquito repellent of the day consisted of smearing bear grease all over the body. The effectiveness of this treatment is not recorded.

Despite these hardships, Pomp seems to have been a happy child. Clark affectionately dubbed him his "little dancing boy." One can imagine the diversion provided by having a child in camp. Native children were trained very early not to be fussy or noisy, so we may assume Pomp's presence on the Expedition did not irritate or inconvenience the Corps's members to

89

any degree. Instead, Clark–in particular–seems to have been genuinely fond of the child. He even named Pompey's Tower, near present-day Billings, Montana, after Sacagawea's son. In addition, a nearby stream was named Baptiste's Creek, which may also have been in honor of Pomp.

When the Corps returned to the Mandan villages in August 1806, Clark asked Charbonneau to let Pomp return to St. Louis with him. Clark said he would raise the boy as his own; he would see that Pomp received the proper schooling along with the opportunity to learn white men's ways. Pomp was barely eighteen months old at this time, and was still being breast fed. The offer was put off until a later time.

Six years later, Charbonneau delivered his sons to Clark in St. Louis. Some oral traditions state he also delivered Pomp's sister, Lizette, to Clark at this time. Clark made good on his offer to raise Pomp with all the advantages Clark's station afforded. Pomp's education was carried out by Catholic and Baptist missionaries. Some time after, he returned to the frontier life as a trader/trapper like his father.

When Pomp was eighteen, he met Prince Paul Wilhelm of Wuertemberg, Germany, who was on a scientific tour of America. Jean Baptiste's unique blend of frontier skills and classical education appealed very much to the prince, who offered to become the young man's patron. Jean Baptiste accepted. He traveled back to Europe with the prince and spent six years as a guest of the royal court. There, he became fluent in at least four more languages and acquired the cultural polish that would set him apart on the Western frontier for the rest of his life. He spoke English, French, German, Spanish, as well as many Native American languages. Jean Baptiste Charbonneau acquired an education far beyond most men of that time.

Upon his return to America in 1829, Jean Baptiste Charbonneau dove wholeheartedly into the mountain man lifestyle. He traveled widely–hunting, trapping, trading, guiding, exploring. He rode with famous frontiersmen, such as Jim Bridger and Kit Carson. According to the Charbonneau family, John C. Frémont was said to have favored Jean Baptiste Charbonneau's boiled buffalo tongue and mint juleps.

During the Mexican War (1846-7), Jean Baptiste served as a scout and guide for the Mormon Battalion of the US Army, leading them from New Mexico to California. Later, he was appointed Alcalde of San Luis Rey Mission, a position of considerable importance. As Alcalde, he served as mayor, justice of the peace, and chief administrator of the law. One of his first acts was to establish an Indian school.

After a time, Jean Baptiste found himself ridiculed by non-natives for "treating the Indians too fairly." Disillusioned by the blatant racism of non-native landowners, and disgusted by the abuses the natives suffered, he finally resigned his position at the mission. He packed his bags and headed toward the gold fields of the California Gold Rush.

Written records reveal him in Auburn, California by 1861, working as a hotel desk clerk. With eyes set on gold-strike towns in Montana, he apparently left Auburn in the spring of 1866. He never made it.

Here, the controversy begins.

Most scholars and historians say that on March 14, 1866, Jean Baptiste Charbonneau died of pneumonia at a tiny stage stop called Innskip Station, near the settlement of Danner, Jordan Valley in remote southeastern Oregon. Records show that this person was buried across the road from Innskip Station in a make-shift graveyard. Today there are several plaques to that effect placed inside the graveyard, plus an Oregon Historical Storyboard (aka "Beaver Board") that identifies Jean Baptiste Charbonneau as Sacagawea's son, and states that his remains are buried in this cemetery.

Oral tradition, however, holds that Jean Baptiste Charbonneau died on the Wind River Indian Reservation in 1885, and was given back to the Earth in the Wind River mountain range, in keeping with tribal custom. His granite memorial headstone stands there, alongside the grave marker of Sacagawea.

Other family traditions state that Jean Baptiste lived to be a very old man, dying in 1903 at the age of ninety-eight, and leaving many descendants.

Captain Meriwether Lewis

The leader of the Corps of Discovery was born August 18, 1774, into the landed gentry of Albemarle County, Virginia, just a few miles from Monticello–home of Thomas Jefferson. Jefferson knew the Lewis family well. Lewis's father had served in the Continental Army and was killed in a horse accident when Lewis was but five years old. A short time later, Lewis's mother was remarried–to another army officer. Lewis was raised on his family's one thousand-acre plantation and educated according to his station. In addition to his scientific and literary studies, Lewis no doubt learned about plants and their medicinal qualities from his mother, an acclaimed herbalist in the region. He joined the Army at the age of twenty and, by 1800, rose to the rank of Captain. The following year President Jefferson appointed Lewis as his personal secretary, intending to mold him for the grand exploration that Jefferson already envisioned.

Lewis, like Jefferson, was tall and thin in stature. He was, from all contemporary accounts, a superb physical specimen. He had a keen eye for detail, and developed a mastery of words (if

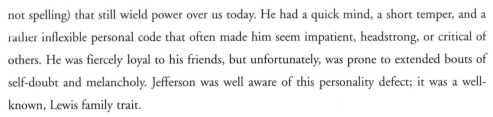

not spelling) that still wield power over us today. He had a quick mind, a short temper, and a rather inflexible personal code that often made him seem impatient, headstrong, or critical of others. He was fiercely loyal to his friends, but unfortunately, was prone to extended bouts of self-doubt and melancholy. Jefferson was well aware of this personality defect; it was a well-known, Lewis family trait.

Both Lewis and Jefferson chose William Clark as co-commander of the Corps of Discovery, but only after Clark's older brother–Revolutionary War hero George Rogers Clark–turned down the job. Oral tradition holds that it was George who suggested his younger brother for the position. Lewis had served in the Army under William Clark for a time, and thought him an excellent choice. Lewis and President Jefferson offered the younger Clark a promotion to captain, should he agree, which would give the co-commanders equal rank and equal authority. Clark accepted.

Jefferson imposed both the heaviest burdens and the highest honors on Meriwether Lewis, who was primarily responsible for putting together the members of the Expedition. Lewis also acted as the party's chief diplomatic officer in the Corps's dealings with native peoples. One gets the feeling in reading the Expedition journals that, although Lewis and Clark were officially equals, Lewis was frequently "more equal" than Clark. To his credit, the journals also show that Lewis often considered the opinions of his men and took advantage of their expertise. Unlike many Army officers of the day, he did occasionally become "one of the boys," hauling his own pack, cooking for the camp, and generally allowing his "rank barrier" to relax a bit. There is no doubt that he was respected and esteemed by his men. What Sacagawea thought of him, we do not know. For Lewis's part, his words reflect a pronounced detachment toward her. She was useful–that was all.

The return journey of the Corps of Discovery in 1806 mark a distinct change in Lewis's demeanor. His melancholy surfaces more frequently. His actions, as related by the journals, often seem overly harsh. Rigid. Rash. Haughtiness and anger seem to overpower Lewis's better judgement. He kills two Blackfeet tribesmen in a skirmish that should never have escalated to that point. In so doing, Lewis commits more than just an impetuous and appalling lack of self-control. His violence sets into motion a Blackfoot blood-feud against the whites that will bring vengeance and retribution to both sides for generations.

In September 1806, when Lewis ended his journey in St. Louis, he was hailed as a bonafide US hero. His accomplishments were, indeed, legion. He and Clark became society's darlings. President Jefferson rewarded Lewis with $1,228 (double pay) and a grant for 1,600 acres of land. The next year, Jefferson appointed him Governor of the Louisiana Territory.

The strain of putting together his Expedition reports and journals for President Jefferson did, however, lead to trouble. Three years in the wilderness had changed Lewis. In the wilderness, he had the focus of one primary mission: to find a waterway through the mountains to the Pacific. In the wilderness, he had a corps of men completely dedicated to him, responsive to his orders, deferential to his leadership. All was structured; all made sense. Now, back in polite society, he was subject to expectations that seemed beyond his control. Pressure to complete reports. Pressure to get the journals published. Scrutiny from every side. Lewis no longer felt like the heroic leader. He was a famous, beleaguered bureaucrat—that was all. Lewis turned to procrastination and heavy drinking.

When the War and Treasury Departments called into question some of Lewis's official expenses, he was asked to come to Washington, DC, to defend himself. He never made it. On October 11, 1809, Lewis was found at an inn called Grinder's Stand on Tennessee's Natchez Trace—dead from a gunshot wound. He was thirty-five years old. Clark believed Lewis shot himself. Most modern historians agree.

Lewis's grave is located next to the inn site in modern-day Meriwether Lewis Park, Tennessee. Today it is marked by a plaque and monument dedicated in 1846. The shaft of the monument rises from its pedestal like a red granite tree trunk, sheared off abruptly midway—a classical reference to a good life, cut short.

Captain William Clark

Born August 1, 1770, William Clark was older than Meriwether Lewis by four years, almost to the day. Originally, Clark's family had been from the same region of Virginia as the Lewis and Jefferson families. However, prior to William's birth, the Clarks moved across the Rappahannock River and set up the homestead where William was born. All of his brothers were Revolutionary War veterans, including war hero George Rogers Clark, who commanded Virginia's troops when Jefferson was Governor of Virginia. Jefferson knew the family well.

William Clark's formative years were spent on the move, finally taking root near Louisville, Kentucky. From there, Clark entered the military with an eye toward a career. He was nineteen. By the time Clark had attained Captain status, Ensign Meriwether Lewis had come under his command. The two became friends. It was a good beginning.

Clark, like Lewis and Jefferson, was over six feet tall and well-built. Though he had far less formal schooling than Lewis, his powers of observation and ability to record what he saw were no less keen. His journals are filled with sketches, maps, and verbal descriptions that make vivid mental pictures even now.

When Clark accepted the solicitation to come out of army retirement and become a co-commander of the Corps of Discovery, he was assured by both Lewis and Jefferson that his rank would be equal to that of Lewis. Under these terms, he agreed, saying to Lewis, "I assure you no man lives with whom I would prefer to undertake such a trip . . . as yourself." Both went forth in good faith that the issue of rank was settled. But when Clark finally received word of his commission on May 7, 1804, it was as Second Lieutenant in the Corps of Artillerists. Lewis was appalled at Jefferson's blatant breach of promise. For over six months—from the time Clark had physically joined the Expedition—he had been addressed as "Captain," and certainly had exercised the authority of that position. Lewis upheld his promise of equality to Clark throughout the Expedition and never revealed to the men that Clark was, in fact, not a captain. After the Expedition, Lewis fought long and hard to have Clark officially recognized as equal in rank to himself and to have Clark's "reward" for the journey be equal to Lewis's own.

Of the two leaders, Clark seems to have had a more personal regard for Sacagawea, Charbonneau, and Pomp. Though he never seems to forget his master/slave relationship with York, Clark does appear to show consideration and affection for Sacagawea and, especially, Pomp. It was Clark who named Pompey's Tower after Sacagawea's son. It was Clark who wrote letters of reference for Charbonneau after the Expedition, and wanted to take Pomp, "my little dancing boy, Baptiste," to raise "as my own son." It was Clark who wrote to Charbonneau that, "Your woman, who accompanied you [on] that long, dangerous, and fatiguing route to the Pacific Ocean and back, deserved a greater reward for her attention and services on that route than we had in our power to give her. . . ."

As it eventually did come to pass, Clark applied for formal guardianship of Pomp, Toussaint (Jr.), and Lizette Charbonneau long after the Expedition. It was Clark who cited Sacagawea as "Dead" in his 1825–8 journal.

Clark's reward for his service in the Corps of Discovery amounted to $1,228 (double pay) and a warrant for 1,600 acres of land. In these things, he was, indeed equal in rank to Lewis. Clark also was given, by a grateful President Jefferson, a double appointment as Brigadier General of Militia, and Superintendent of Indian Affairs for the Territory of Upper Louisiana. These titles were put into effect the year after the Corps' successful return to St. Louis.

The following year, Clark married his long-time sweetheart, Julia Hancock (also called "Judith"), after whom he named a river. He named one of their sons Meriwether Lewis Clark.

After Lewis's death, Clark collaborated with Nicholas Biddle on the publication of the Expedition journals. Much of the material from Biddle's interviews with Clark appear in the final version; the original journals do not always reflect this information.

In 1813, ten years after Clark embarked upon his greatest voyage of discovery, he was named Governor of the Missouri Territory, a post he held until 1820. After the death of his wife Judith, Clark married again. He continued to serve as Superintendent of Indian Affairs, and apparently earned the respect of the native peoples, trappers, and traders whose business he oversaw. He spent the remainder of his life in service to his family and his country, dying at age sixty-eight in St. Louis.

Clark is buried in Bellefontaine Cemetery in St. Louis, near the Missouri River. His monument includes a stately white obelisk, and a bust of Clark as Statesman. The inscription reads, "Soldier, Explorer, Statesman, and Patriot. His Life Is Written In The History Of His Country."

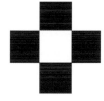

York, slave of William Clark

In his will, Clark's father bequeathed York to William Clark. York and Clark were roughly the same age, so probably grew up together, albeit separated by their slave/owner relationship. He was married at the time of the Expedition, but his wife had been sold to a different owner who lived near Louisville. We know York only by that one name. Typically, when slaves were sold, they were listed on the sales roster with the last names of their owners. For York, this practice was apparently not followed.

We know from the journals that he was a big, well-formed black man of considerable strength. Not only did he provide much-needed physical labor in the camps, he was also a focal point of amazement and delight for the native peoples. He was considered by the tribes to be "Big Medicine," a being of special prowess and power. The color of York's skin, his strength, and the texture of his hair made many think he must be part buffalo, or that he shared the buffalo's Spirit. The native word for "York," in some languages of the upper Missouri, translated to "Black White Man." In the words of a contemporary account, "despite his ebony complexion, [York] was looked upon with decided partiality, and received his share of adulation" during the journey.

It is known that York could swim, unlike some of the Corpsmen, including Charbonneau. He was recorded as being a good hunter. We know, therefore, that he carried a weapon during the journey and was expected to use it. Had York and Clark been back home in "the U. States," York, as a slave, would have been prohibited from carrying a weapon of any kind.

York was given the opportunity to officially voice his opinion as to where Fort Clatsop should be built. Thus, he was allowed to "vote," another example of the wilderness functioning as the great equalizer. York became the first African-American known to have crossed the continental United States. In Clark's listing of creeks and rivers named by both captains, there is an entry for "York's 8 Islands," located somewhere along the Missouri River in present-day Montana. As with so many of the names Lewis and Clark conferred on the land, this one faded into history.

As Clark's manservant, York was expected to be at his side unless ordered elsewhere. This obligation extended to the living and sleeping arrangements on the journey. As a result of these expectations, York was privileged; the captain's quarters tended to be the best of the camp. It must have been a strange situation for York: on the one hand, treated almost as a free and equal man by the Corps; on the other, never able to escape the fact that he was a slave, the property of Captain Clark.

After the Expedition, when York returned with Clark to normal daily life, he petitioned Clark for his freedom. Clark refused. York asked to be hired out to the owner of his wife Rose so they could be together. Clark, in words gleaned from his journal, reprimanded York for

being "insolent and sulky," and had him beaten. Three years later, he relented and sent York to Kentucky.

It was not until some ten years later that Clark freed York and outfitted him with a wagon and six horses. According to Clark, York started a freight line company between Richmond and Nashville, but proved to be such a bad businessman that he lost the entire enterprise. He was returning to Clark, the story goes, when he died of cholera somewhere in Tennessee. Some oral traditions maintain that York, when granted his freedom, returned to the West where he settled among the Crow Indians and became an honored warrior.

William Bratton was born in Virginia in 1778, to parents of Irish descent. He was four years younger than Lewis, eight years younger than Clark. Having moved to Kentucky with his parents when he was about twelve years old, Bratton was considered a Kentuckian. He became an accomplished blacksmith and gunsmith before setting out with the Corps of Discovery. Bratton was one of the men assigned to the salt works on the Pacific Coast during that long, wet winter at Fort Clatsop. There, he developed severe rheumatism in his back that crippled him with pain. Lewis doubted he would ever recover. On the Corps' return trip, Bratton's leg and back pain were successfully treated by the Nez Perce with traditional sweat baths.

Compared with his compatriots, Bratton married rather late in life (at age forty-one), thirteen years after his expedition with Lewis and Clark. He sired eight sons and two daughters, a family of typical size for that time, before he died in 1841 at age sixty-three.

Private John Collins

We do not know the exact date of John Collins' birth; we do know that he came from Frederick County, Maryland. He was already in an army unit when his name was transferred to the official Expedition muster roll. As a skilled hunter, he was much valued on the journey. He was also occasionally pressed into service as camp cook.

He was one of the first of the Corps to be hauled before its formal disciplinary trial process. His charge: getting drunk while on guard duty. Both he and Hugh Hall tapped the whiskey barrel that was put under their guard for the night. Collins was found guilty and sentenced to a punishment of one hundred lashes on his bare back.

Private John Colter

John Colter was born in Augusta County, Virginia, about the same time as Meriwether Lewis. (The best estimates put the year of Colter's birth as 1775.) At approximately five years of age, he moved to Kentucky with his family, so he considered himself a Kentuckian. An astute frontiersman of note, Colter excelled as a hunter and was a keen observer of the land. These qualities made him invaluable to the Corps of Discovery. Colter was in his late twenties when he traveled to the Pacific Ocean with Lewis and Clark.

Upon returning with them to the Mandan Villages in August 1806, Colter requested–and was granted–an "early out" from his military duties. This early discharge enabled him to join two Illinois trappers in setting up their own fur business; they trapped the very rivers Colter had just explored with the Corps.

Several years later, he and former Corps member John Potts were trapping in Blackfoot country when the two men were captured. Potts was killed. Colter was shot through with so many arrows that he described himself as being "made a riddle of." After much discussion as to how they would kill him, the Blackfeet finally decided to strip Colter naked and make him race for his life. If caught, Colter would instantly die. If he succeeded in outrunning and outwitting his captors, his life would be his own. Odds, clearly, were not on Colter's side. He ran naked and weaponless for eleven days, carrying only the blanket and spear he'd stolen when he killed one of his pursuers. He hid in beaver mounds, rock slides, and snow caves; he ate roots, tree bark, and leaves. When he finally staggered into Fort Manuel on the Big Horn, he had covered over three hundred miles. John Colter survived, and his reputation for courage and resourcefulness was forever fixed.

From about 1811 to 1813, Colter is known to have tried his hand at farming with "Sallie," his native wife, but apparently did not give up his wandering ways. He is credited with being the first non-native to enter and explore what is today Yellowstone National Park. When he described the geysers, boiling mud holes, mineral flows, and other geothermal phenomena of the area, listeners dubbed it "Colter's Hell," which only cemented the legend of this already larger-than-life mountain man who actually stood just five feet ten inches tall.

Private Pierre Cruzatte

Listed by Lewis as "Peter" Cruzatte in the Corps list of April 7, 1805, this trader/trapper was of French and Omaha Indian blood. He was skilled in sign language and served as an inter-

preter during his tenure in the Corps. He was also an expert boatman. His violin playing enlivened many a camp night during the journey and must have offered an interesting contrast to the native drumming and singing that accompanied the Corps down the Columbia River.

Dubbed "St. Peter" by others on the Expedition, Cruzatte had only one good–albeit, near-sighted–eye. Not surprisingly, it was he who (presumably) mistook Lewis for an elk in August 1806, and shot him, wounding the captain in the buttocks and thigh. In his 1825-8 journal, Clark lists Cruzatte as dead.

George Drouillard

This man's last name is also frequently spelled "Drewyer" in the journals. Born in Canada to a French father and Shawnee mother, he served as interpreter for the Expedition. Drouillard kept his civilian status within the Corps of Discovery and, as such, earned a stipend of twenty-five dollars per month. He was highly skilled in the use of sign language. Lewis considered him the best hunter in the Corps and seems to have been highly confident in Drouillard's ability to "read the land." Drouillard accompanied Lewis into the Shoshoni camp ahead of Clark, Sacagawea, Charbonneau, and the others. There, he used his knowledge of sign language to facilitate Lewis's communication with the tribe.

When the Corps returned to St. Louis on September 23, 1806, Drouillard was entrusted with the delivery of Lewis's first letters and reports to the postmaster in Cahokia, who, in turn, was to forward them to President Jefferson. Later, Drouillard returned to the Three Forks region as a member of Manuel Lisa's fur trading party. He was killed there by the Blackfeet in 1810.

Privates Joseph Fields and Reuben Fields

These brothers were born two years apart in the mid-1770s in Culpepper County, Virginia. They later moved to Kentucky. The Fields brothers were two of the earliest to enlist in the Expedition. Outstanding hunters and woodsmen, they were often chosen to act as scouts. Reuben was recorded as an excellent runner; Joseph built rough-hewn writing desks for the captains at Fort Clatsop.

On the return journey, both Fields brothers accompanied Lewis on his exploration of the Marias River. It was during this trek that two Blackfeet were killed in a skirmish with the Corps. The site is near present-day Cut Bank, Montana.

Both Joseph and Reuben were discharged upon completion of the Corps' mission, at which time Lewis praised them most highly. Reuben eventually died in Kentucky. Joseph took a military land grant in Franklin, Missouri.

Private Robert Frazier

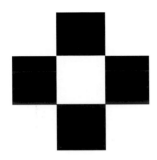

This Virginian, like Bratton and Colter, was born in Augusta County. Originally listed in Clark's Orderly Book as a member of the "Extra Party," Frazier was transferred to the "Permanent Party" in October 1804, to replace Moses Reed who had been dismissed for attempted desertion.

Frazier kept a journal during the Expedition. He asked for, and received, permission from the captains to have it published, but scholars today say the journal never made it to press. The whereabouts of the original journal is not known. Frazier did, however, publish a "teaser" of the larger prospective work which states that as soon as he had "sufficient subscriptions to defray the expenses," he anticipated publication of a four-hundred-page tome. The price of each subscription was three dollars. Presumably, subscribers were too few to fund his book.

Frazier eventually became a fencing master in Battleborough, Vermont. He died in 1837 in Franklin County, Missouri.

Sergeant Patrick Gass

Patrick Gass was born in Falling Springs, Pennsylvania in 1771. He joined the army at age eighteen. He was serving at Kaskaskia, Illinois Territory when the edict from the Secretary of War ordered Gass's commander to supply the Corps of Discovery with "one Sergeant and eight good men." Gass was eager to go, but his commanding officer at Kaskaskia was reluctant to lose his skills in carpentry and woodworking. Gass made a personal plea to Captain Lewis, who interceded for him, and secured his transfer to the Corps as one of the "eight good men." Upon the death of Sergeant Floyd, Gass was elected to fill the then-vacant slot of sergeant.

Even though Gass admitted he had not learned to "read, write, or cipher" until he was an adult, his Expedition journals provide added perspective on events both monumental and mundane. The 1807 journal, published under Gass's name, was actually the result of his collaboration with a Pittsburgh editor named McKeehan. It was the first official account of the Expedition to be published.

Gass went on to serve in the US Infantry during the War of 1812. At the age of sixty, he married Maria Hamilton and had seven children. When he died in 1870, he was ninety-nine years old. His grave sits high on a hill in Brooke Cemetery, West Virginia.

Private George Gibson

We know George Gibson was born in Pennsylvania; we do not know when. Captain Clark lists him as a Kentuckian so, evidently, Gibson had lived in Kentucky for some time before his enlistment into the Corps. He was a skilled woodsman and an excellent marksman. He also had some musical ability and experience with sign language. Gibson died in St. Louis only three years after the Corps' triumphant 1806 return.

Private Silas Goodrich

The life of this Massachusetts-born member of the Corps is a mystery, both before and after the time his service with Lewis and Clark. The journals tout his reputation as a fine fisherman; otherwise, his activities and assignments appear to be routine. Clark lists Goodrich as being deceased by 1825.

Private Hugh Hall

There is some disagreement as to whether Hugh Hall was born in Carlisle, Pennsylvania, or somewhere in Massachusetts, but the year seems fixed: 1772. He was "regular army," having enlisted in 1798. It was Hall who joined John Collins in getting drunk on guard duty during the Expedition. Though Hall seems to have liked his liquor over-well and, consequently, ended up in a variety of disciplinary scrapes, he stayed the full distance with the Corps. We lose track of him completely after the Expedition.

Private Thomas P. Howard

Thomas Howard was born in Brimfield, Massachusetts, in 1779. When he was twenty-two years old, he enlisted in the army. He joined the Lewis and Clark Expedition three years later. It is recorded that Clark said of him, "Howard never drinks water." We take this to mean that Howard–like Hall–enjoyed his liquor.

It should be noted that liquor was regulation-issue in most military actions of the day. Its absence, according to the journals, was keenly felt on certain legs of the Corps' journey.

Howard, however, does seem to push the rules more than most. He is listed as having been apprehended scaling the Fort Mandan palisade on his return from a forbidden, after-hours visit to the Mandan villages.

We do know that he married after the Expedition and had a son who lived in St. Louis. Clark's 1825-8 listing of Expedition members, and their whereabouts, does not include Howard.

Private François LaBiche

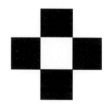

The year of LaBiche's birth is not known, only that he was born to a French father and Omaha Indian mother. His native language skills were superb, as was his experience with sign language, trading, bartering, and the management of the boats. Because LaBiche was conversant in both French and English, he was often pressed to translate for Lewis and Clark. It was LaBiche who provided the critical link between the captains and Charbonneau (and, therefore, to Sacagawea) during negotiations with the Shoshones. Wherever Lewis is found on the journey, there also is LaBiche.

After the Expedition, LaBiche and Sergeant Ordway were tasked with escorting a pack train bound for President Jefferson, laden with all manner of specimens gathered by Lewis and Clark on their voyage of discovery. The last record we have of LaBiche is from Clark's journal; it indicates he was living in the St. Louis area around 1825.

Private Jean Baptiste LePage

Jean Baptiste LePage was living among the Minnetaree (Hidatsa) and Mandan Indians when Lewis and Clark first met him. He, like Charbonneau, was a French-Canadian trapper. Evidently he was recruited into the Corps to fill the gap left by John Newman's discharge.

At the end of the Expedition, when the War Department was tallying pay for those who had participated, LePage was allotted two-thirds as much as the other permanent Corps members as he had served only from the point of his recruitment at the Mandan Villages. His life, both before and after the Expedition, is a mystery.

Private Hugh McNeal

We know Hugh McNeal was born and raised in Pennsylvania, that he was entered into the "Permanent Party" roll of the Corps on April 1, 1804, and that after the Expedition and just prior to the War of 1812, he served in the Infantry. During the journey, his most questionable claim to fame involved the sneaking off with a native man in the middle of the night (during the Clatsop winter) to look for female companionship. Clark's journal, however, opines that McNeal had been duped, and, in truth, the natives intended to kill McNeal for his blanket and clothing. At any rate, a serious fight broke out between the Corpsmen and the natives. Afterward, McNeal was returned to camp. He seems to have served to the end of the Expedition without much further incident.

Clark's list of those living and deceased, written twenty years later between 1825 and 1828, indicates that McNeal was thought to be dead by that time.

Private John Ordway

Born and educated in New Hampshire, John Ordway was in his late twenties when he was made a permanent member of the Corps. His schooling went beyond the norm of the day. He had an eye for detail and an ear for words, both of which make his Expedition journals interesting to read. Ordway was given many administrative responsibilities on the journey: keeping the registers and records; assigning guard duties; issuing provisions; and, assuming command in the captains' absence. This last duty seems not to have been his forte, for many violations of orderly conduct by the men seemed to take place during his pro-tem commands.

After the Expedition, Lewis and Clark agreed to buy publishing rights to Ordway's journal and incorporate its contents into their own book. They paid him $300. In addition, Ordway was given double pay for his participation in the Expedition and 320 acres of Missouri farm land. He seems to have lived the remainder of his life on the land, dying unmarried and childless around 1817.

Private John Potts

John Potts was born in Germany about the time the United States declared its independence from Great Britain. He immigrated to America (whether alone or with his family is not known) where he worked in a grist mill. In his mid-twenties, he joined the army. He was serving in Tennessee when Lewis and Clark recruited him to join the Corps of Discovery.

After the Expedition, Potts joined the Manuel Lisa fur trading party that was headquartered along the upper Missouri River. John Colter was a member of Lisa's group at the same time. Potts and Colter were captured by the Blackfeet near the Three Forks in 1810. Colter escaped with his life. Potts did not.

Sergeant Nathaniel Pryor

Born in Virginia in 1772, Nathaniel Pryor moved to Kentucky when he was eleven years old. There he came to manhood, married in 1798, and eventually became a member of the Lewis and Clark Expedition. He was a cousin to Charles Floyd—the only Corpsman to die on the eight thousand mile journey. When Floyd died, Pryor was given his personal effects.

Like Sergeants Gass and Ordway, Pryor was given much responsibility on the Expedition. He was generally considered an able man of character and reliability; his name appears often in the journals of both Lewis and Clark. The Captains even named a river for him.

Pryor was one of the men who accompanied Clark on the return trip via the Yellowstone River. He and four others in the party constructed Mandan-style "bull boats"—boats made of buffalo hides stretched over willow frames—and paddled them to the rendezvous point on the Missouri River. Unfortunately, Pryor had dislocated his shoulder earlier in the Expedition. Through much effort and exertion it was "popped" back into place, but the shoulder would plague Pryor for the rest of his life—a painful reminder of the journey.

After his adventures with Lewis and Clark, Pryor settled with the Osage Indians; he married again and had a family. (No record was found as to what became of his first wife.) In tribal negotiations with Fort Smith and Fort Gibson, Pryor acted as the tribe's representative. He was even appointed by Clark—then, the Superintendent of Indian Affairs—as sub-agent for the Osage Clermont band. Pryor died among his Osage people at age fifty-nine.

Private George Shannon

George Shannon was only eighteen, the youngest of the Corps, when he was recruited by Captain Lewis to join the Expedition. Though born in Pennsylvania, Shannon had been going to school in Kentucky, where the Governor was a relative of his. Shannon's parents, however, still lived in Pennsylvania; it was here he met Lewis and learned of the upcoming Expedition.

When he enlisted, he was designated second in command to Sergeant Pryor's squad. His city upbringing and privileged schooling did not prepare him for the wilderness. In the journals, Shannon seems most often to be lost, or his whereabouts unaccounted for. He also had difficulty with unfamiliar hand-and-tool work, cutting or otherwise injuring himself in either process. One assumes that Shannon eventually mastered the necessary wilderness survival skills, and that his status as "tenderfoot" changed with experience. On the return journey, Clark thought highly enough of the young man to name "Shannon's Creek" after him.

Private John Shields

John Shields was another son of Augusta County, Virginia, who migrated to Kentucky. He, like Pryor, was a married man when Lewis and Clark recruited him for the Expedition. His skills as a blacksmith and gunsmith proved invaluable to the Corps, and he was often praised in the captains' journals for his ingenuity. Shields's name was given to a stream and a river in what is, now, Montana. After the Expedition, Lewis recommended that the Secretary of War grant Shields additional reward in payment for his vital services—another indication of the captains' high regard for Shields.

What became of Shields' family in his absence, we do not know. Some records seem to indicate he married a second time in 1808.

Private John Thompson

Very little is known about John Thompson's life both before, and after the Lewis and Clark Expedition. Records indicate he was, at one time, a surveyor in Vincennes, Indiana. Certainly this would have been a skill useful to the Corps of Discovery. Clark's 1825–8 listing of those Corps members living and dead, simply lists Thompson as "killed" by that time.

Private Peter Weiser

This name is frequently spelled "Wiser" in the journals. Peter Weiser was born in Pennsylvania in 1781. He was already in the army when Lewis and Clark recruited him for the Corps of Discovery. Apparently, the captains named the Weiser River in western Idaho after him. The modern-day town of Weiser, Idaho, on the Snake River is likewise named in his honor.

He is known to have been active in the fur trade after the Expedition. Oral histories have him traveling widely across the West, beyond the Continental Divide. Clark's 1825–8 list of those living and those deceased describes Peter Weiser as "killed."

Private William Werner

Werner appears out of nowhere in the winter of 1803/1804, already a member of the Corps. There is some indication that he was born in Kentucky, but no confirming evidence exists. He was a scrapper, noted in the journals as having to be disciplined for fighting and being absent without leave. Other than this, his service appears to have been routine.

At this time, many Kentuckians had the reputation of being wilderness-wise and survival-savvy. Perhaps this was Werner's appeal to the captains. Twenty-some years after the Expedition–when Clark was Superintendent of Indian Affairs–Werner served under him as an Indian agent for a time. That is the last we hear of him.

Private Joseph Whitehouse

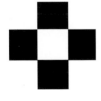

Born about 1775 in Fairfax County, Virginia, Joseph Whitehouse and his family moved to Kentucky when he was close to nine years old. He enlisted in the army at the age of twenty-three, served his regular five-year term, and then "re-upped." It was during his second hitch in the army that Lewis and Clark chose him to be a member of the Corps. He was known as a good skin dresser and tailor, skills that would be vital during the journey. He also kept a journal, eventually published as part of the Reuben Thwaites interpretation of the Lewis and Clark journals.

After the Expedition, he received his discharge, $166.67 in pay, and the promised land grant. He sold the land to his former Corps-mate, George Drouillard. The following year, Whitehouse was arrested for debt in Missouri. This downturn hastened his re-enlistment into the army, where he served through the War of 1812 as a career soldier until his desertion in 1817.

Private Alexander Willard

Alexander Willard was born in New Hampshire the year after the Declaration of Independence was signed. When he enlisted in the army at the age of twenty-two, he listed himself as a Kentuckian. He, like John Shields, was a blacksmith and gunsmith by trade.

Lewis and Clark designated him as Shields' assistant. On the journey, he was tried and convicted under martial law, of sleeping on sentry duty–a crime punishable by death. Instead, he was sentenced to a whipping of one hundred lashes and kept as a permanent member of the Corps.

After the Expedition, Willard married and had a family of seven sons and five daughters. He and his family later emigrated to California by covered wagon. He died near Sacramento, California, just before the end of the Civil War.

Richard Windsor

Richard Windsor is another of the Corps' mystery men. We know he enlisted into the army from Kentucky and joined the Corps at Camp Dubois on New Year's Day, 1804. He seems to have been an experienced woodsman and able hunter on the journey. He served without either positive or negative distinction.

After the Expedition, he apparently took up residence on the Sangamon River in Illinois, as recorded in Clark's 1825–8 roster of those Corps members believed to be living or dead.

******

Sergeant Charles Floyd

Though Floyd died prior to Sacagawea's entrance onto the Corps of Discovery's stage, his dubious claim to fame is as the only Corps member on the Expedition to die in its service. He was one of the first to volunteer for service, and was judged by Clark to be a "man of much merit." Floyd kept a journal from May 14, 1804 to August 18, 1804–two days before his death from what the captains called, "bilious colic." Modern historians and medical experts define this condition as a ruptured appendix.

He was buried, according to Clark, "with honors of war," on a bluff overlooking what the captains named "Floyd's River." Today, the Sergeant's grave site in Sioux City, Iowa, is a most impressive memorial. The original cedar post placed on Floyd's grave by his compatriots is gone. In its place stands a new marker, dedicated to Floyd's memory in 1901. This one-hundred-foot-high, sandstone obelisk–second only to the Washington Monument in size–punctuates the sky like a gigantic exclamation point.

Shoshoni Vocabulary

The following phonetic rendition of Shoshoni vocabulary (including words, animal names, short phrases, and short statements and questions) is excerpted from the private collection of the Reverend John Roberts, who served as a missionary on the Wind River Indian Reservation for sixty-six years. He began his duties among the Shoshone in 1883; it was Reverend Roberts who officiated at the Christian burial of the woman known as Sacagawea on the Wind River Reservation the following year. Today, there is much scholarly controversy over whether this woman was, indeed, the same person who played such an important role in Lewis and Clark's voyage of discovery. There was no doubt in Reverend Roberts's mind, nor in the minds of most reservation residents.

Today—with renewed interest in traditional tribal culture—the spelling of many of these Shoshoni words has been restructured to more accurately reflect the language as it was spoken. Keep in mind that Reverend Roberts was a non-native, trying—over one hundred years ago—to record unfamiliar sounds.

This vocabulary appears with the kind permission of Reverend Roberts's granddaughter, Beatrice Crofts, of Lander, Wyoming.

Short Shoshoni Phrases

ask her	ma-ruv-ve
a high place	bahint
a hunting place	dam-dehoowe-gar
a rocky place	sont-din-he-gant
a shady place	hig-e-a-chant
a fishing place	dam-be-ngua-gar
eagle nest	gwana-ungan
I see	nia-a-awik
in the meadow grasses	shoshoni daint
in the woods	soho-gav
lead your horse	im-bun-sang-uk-u
looking toward sunrise	dabe-un-do-ik-a-vooik
looking toward sunset	dabe-you-ic-megar-booit
on the cliff	dim-ba-nach
on the shore	bea-va-un-gu-math-ogwie-un-gunach
place to eat	ish-bing-a-yooint-yn-dig-a
place to rest	ish-pin-ga-yoont

the summer camp	dats-un-gan
when friends meet	dan-hanch-na-wagar
where berries grow	Se-bo-hoom-segan
where the birds sing	hoo-joo-un-dinooe-gar
where flowers grow	booip-sea-gan
you see	yn-awik

Shoshoni Statements and Questions

Are you better?	Yn ha san na hun?
Are you sick?	Yn ha nidzik?
Give me a horse.	Na vongu mak.
Go and get it.	Nuk meak.
I did not sleep.	Ne a ga-ep-wi.
I have lost my horse	Nea ratz na vong ne wad-zi.
I want some water.	Oa its-sue.
I will speak to her.	Nia ma ma an deg aro.
It is enough.	Sov ve gesh.
Light a fire.	Ma guto.
Put it here.	Hik mar ik.
Tell him to come.	Ma raru.
What is your name?	Haga yn naniak?
When will you come?	In himba gim hond?
Whose lodge is this?	Tish hock en gan ne?

Shoshoni Words (circa 1883)

above	ba-hn
across	o-ha-ro
afraid	ma-ree-e-ent
angry	to-ho-vwk
arm	be-yr
ask	or-riv-vi
axe	ho-wan-ni

basket	se-ah-woush
beads	tsome
beans	pe-hw-rah
beautiful	san-na-vwint/ san-nab-oon-ie

beaver skin	em-poo
beaver trap	han-ny-wun
before	gist-hi-e-gan
belt	nic
big	pe-up/ be-at-che
big man	bi-ar-in-appwe
big water	bea-ba
bite	na-goo-sho-nip
bitter	mo-ats
black	tw-hw-vit
blanket	nav-o-eeh
blood	purp
blue	tve-we-bit
boat	suck
boats	suck-i
bone	tson-ip
born	pa-han
bow	ho-ate
braid hair	nar-an-gush-ek
brass kettle	awe-wit-too
bread	tos-te-cup
bring	mei-ak
bring to	sho-gope-ma-yack
buckskin	yes-im-bit
buffalo robe	kootch-en-empoo
burn, to	ma-go-too
buttons	tay-toom-buck-ah

candle	yupe-te-gup-pe-tor/ coo-net-se-ah
carry it along	ma-zah-yah
catch	mah-mah-me-gum-mah/ mat-siah
chew	mo-git-so-whin
chief	cop-e-tah/ le-gwan-i
close, near	ne-tit-se
cold	id-jen
cook	guash-up
cooked	bash-up

corn	han-ne-vit
corn meal	han-ne-vit-na-o-sup
council	ne-wis-a-ra
count	mar-rid-zi
count, to	marit-zay
country	sho-go-pe
country, big	man-nunk-so-gwp
cradleboard	ko-no/ ko-na
cry	yag-ut
cups	nar-ak/ nah-rac
cut	ma-zik-ka/mat-se-eah

dance	nic-a-ro
dark	kay-na-vu-e-kent
dawn	o-hah-wan-ig-gi
day	tab-bi
day after tomorrow	pi-no-qua-percn
day before yesterday	hi-e-gan-kint
dead	de-ape
deaf	kay-ming-en
dirt	sho-gup
dismount	way/wah
disobedient	kay-ne-nun-ga-bidge-e
do	ma-han-it
dream	nav-oo-she-ai
drink	mah-hev-v
dry	pash-up

ear	o-nanyk
eat	dic-a-ro-ma-ric
eaten enough	su-be-gus-mar-rick
embrace	ma-gwab
enough	sho-ve-gash
ermine skin	pah-pidge-em-bet
evening	yeak
eye	pw-i

F	fall	ba-heik
	far	na-na-gwr
	fast	nam-ish-a
	fat	youp
	feather	se-ah
	feet	namp
	find	may-ow-rah
	fingers	mo-sho-wie
	fire	wai-ant
	flat	se-a-pa-gant
	flour	to-sho-te-cup
	Frenchman	U-an-te-bo
	friend	hansh/ shih-mas-na-hansh
	funny	nan-as-snom-sum-mite
G	girl	ni-ve/ im-bed-e
	give me	ma-ut
	glass, looking	nav-voo
	go	nook
	go to	me-ar-ro
	good	zant
	grass, dry	shaw-nip
	grass, green	poo-ip
	grease wood	tow-mo-pe
	grieve	dwt-ha-nia-shwn-gar
	gun	pe-ate
H	hair	pam-be-kant
	hand	um-moo-ah
	handkerchief	wan-aga-rook
	happiness	se-nea-shoon-gan
	hard	git-ant
	hat	diz-zong-mo-i
	heart	be-mem-pe
	help	ne-re-ma-zom-mo
	herd	ma-ric-co-on

here	sick/ ig-ish
home	yn-gan-i
hungry	pah-du-ah
hunt	ma-wic
hunting for game	te-ya-guanto
hurt	wm-mar-ra
Indian, Shoshone	Nim-ah
kill	mah-vic/ wig-gar-ro
knife	hab-be-weeh
lake	pah-kah-re
last summer	moom-nan-hua
laugh	yan-a-kin
lead to	ma-zank
leggings	oom-ah-wit-tah-ma
legs	oom
lie down	hobe
lie, untruth	ish-amp
lightning	toom-yac-ah
listen	mo-nun-ga-he
love	nash-um
make	ma-han
man	dun-ap-we
many birds	shont-hoo-joo
many boats	shont-sak
married	peroh-an-gwe-kent
marsh	seg-we-dant
me	ne-ah
meal	han-neep
medicine	nat-a-so
medicine man	bo-ho-gant

middle	un-ach
moccasin	namp
moccasins	pah-nampa
month	sum-mw-mu-ia
moon	mu-ia
morning	be-etch-chws/ pen-che-co
mountain	to-yap-doi-abi
mud	se-gwip

night	to-gan
noon	tog-gwe-tabby
north fork	sho-o-gwap

often	son-na
old woman	hiv-ve-zot-sie
on top	ov-up
one year old	tum-in-dwa

pines	wo-ong-go-pi
pipe	toke-or-to-we
plains	pa-wit-se
plant, to	tim-as-see-in-kin-do
proud	na-van-ah-vite

rain	pah-a-mar
rainbow	pah-o-gwo-a-bit
ran	na-na-area-o
red	ank-a-bit
river	og-wip
rock	timp
round	toom-bo-nate
rub	nash-oi-ip

S

salt	o-na-bit/ toso-o-nap
say	tay-gwe-na
see	bu-wick
seed	te-mah-se-en-gah
shake hands	mo-od-dsai
sick	nid-dzi-guar
sign talk	ma-wo-ya-guin
sinew	iwn-dam
sing	di-nig-huant
skin	peg-up
skin scraper	tes-eep
sky, clear	toot-za-wit
smell	mah-eke
smoke	gwi-ket
snow	tuck-ah-vit
starved to death	con-e-de-ape
steal	ma-rid-ic
stomach	tun-na-ant
stone	tim-by
strong	git-tant
sugar	pee-nah
sweet	pe-nah-ka-munt/ pee-nah-munt

T

talk	ta-guin
tall	giw-vir-ant
teeth	dam-mu
thirsty	da-gwt-tie
thunder	toom-yac-cah
tobacco	bam
today	tab-by
tongue	e-kw
trade	ma-re-mere-o
trail	bo-he
trap	wan-ny
truth	te-bits

e	undecided	tish-u-wan-sip
	understand	shum-ban-ah

w	want	ma-soo-int
	water	pah
	weep	yag-ah
	white	to-sho-bit
	willow	she-her-bit
	wind	toomp/ ne-ate
	woman	wipe
	wood stick	hwp-gwan
	work	dir-ah-i

y	yellow	o-ah-bit
	yesterday	kint
	you	nim

Shoshoni Animal Names

Antelope	Quaritz
Antelope, buck	Wantz
Antelope, skin	Quar-em-poo-e
Bald eagle	Bas-sea
Bear	Wurrah
Bear, black	Doo-wurrah
Bear, brown	Outa-wurrah
Bear, grizzly	Tosa-wurrah
Bear, yellow	Oa-wurrah-agwa
Beaver	Hav-ne
Bobcat	Me-am-be/Se-rook-goc
Buffalo	Kootch
Buffalo Calf	Tuc-wat-se
Coyote	Teah-ish-a-paa
Crane	Wass
Crane, sand	Hillgo-an-dat-ta
Crow	Kak/gak

Deer, buck	Doo-tea
Deer, doe	So-go-rea-un-doo-a
Dog	Sar-re
Elk	Bar-re
Fish	Bek-we
Fox, black	To-wan
Fox, red	O-to-wan-ny/Enga-wd-ne
Geese	Ne-gint
Horse	De-he
Jay bird	Wo-yw-a-de-a
Lynx	Doo-goo-vitch
Mallard	Boo-ye
Mink	Doo-bas-we-bas-saw
Mole	Do-mo-wit-o-gwa
Mountain lion	Do-ya-roo-goo
Mountain sheep	Mu-zam-bi-e
Muskrat	Bam-bw-ka
Otter	Pan-zook
Porcupine	Yi-ir
Prairie Dog	Tind-say
Rabbit	Tap-oot-se
Sage Grouse	Po-ho-gin-no
Salmon	A-gae
Skunk	Bo-ne-ats
Snake	Togo-ah
Sparrow hawk	Ge-ne
Squirrel	Woon-g-rats
Trout	Sa-ben-gwe
Turtle	Bea-yag-wad-sa
Weasel	Pam-pidg-e
Wolf	T-djap-u

1. The term "squaw" is used here as it was in Sacagawea's time, simply meaning "native woman," or more specifically, "a married native woman." The derogatory connotation now associated with the word cannot be proven to be part of the word's etymology. Before European contact, the Narragansett peoples of the eastern seaboard seem to have used their word *squua* to mean "female." This practice was adopted by the early European colonists, and came into common usage among them as a word designating a native woman. There also seems to have been a formal title which the colonists had undoubtedly heard, used between the Narragansett and other coastal Algonkians (aka Algonquians) for their hereditary, female heads of state. This title of respect and honor was *saunck-squua* (sometimes spelled sunksquaw). (See *The Sacred Hoop* by Paula Gunn Allen and *The Making of Sacagawea* by Donna J. Kessler for further discussion of this term's origin.)

2. The meaning of Sacagawea's name is still a matter of some dispute among scholars. Depending upon which language is used, the various spellings of her name alter the meanings. Spelled "Sacajawea" in the Shoshoni language, the name means "Boat Pusher" or "Boat Launcher." In the Hidatsa (Minnetaree) language–with the spelling of "Sakakawea," or more precisely, "Tsakaka-wea"–the meaning becomes "Bird Woman." We are unable to discern from the Corps of Discovery journals precisely what the official spelling should be, as these non-native journal keepers recorded words as their untrained ears heard them. Indeed, there are multiple variations within the same journal, and sometimes within the same entry. Since Lewis states in his journals that the Bird Woman's River was named for the "Snake"-born woman who served as interpreter, scholars generally agree that the Hidatsa version of her name is the closest to being correct. Today, you will find many spellings of the name, depending upon which geographical area of the country you visit. The spelling endorsed and adopted by the US Geographic Board is "Sacagawea."

3. In most native traditions, a person may have a variety of names. Some are familiar. Some are ceremonial. Some are bestowed in honor of certain events or to commemorate crucial and life-altering experiences in that person's life. Others come in a holy way and are not to be spoken of or made public. Names hold power. They bind the clan together and often reflect a person's place within the larger family or tribe. It was common at that time–among Sacagawea's birth people–to acknowledge the transition from "without child" to "having child" by the designation of a new name indicating an enhanced level of status and responsibility within the clan. (See endnote 46.)

4. This is also sometimes spelled "Nuwu-ma" or "Nuwu-na," meaning "The People." "Agui Dika" is sometimes seen as "Aguidika," or "Aguiduka," meaning "Salmon Eaters." Today we refer to this particular group of the Shoshone tribe as the Lemhi Shoshone. Some scholars and some oral traditions have pinpointed Sacagawea's birth place around present-day Salmon, Idaho.

5. The hand sign mistaken for "snake" has also been described as the motion involved in basket weaving, at which the Shoshones excelled. As in so many other things, the name sign used by this tribe was misunderstood by those to whom it was unfamiliar. By the time Lewis and Clark undertook the Expedition, the term "Snake"–referring to those who were also called Shoshone– was firmly established.

6. This topographical landmark can still be seen not far from present-day Dillon, Montana. Local lore echoes Sacagawea's explanation to Lewis that, to her tribe, the face and top of the formation looked like the top of a beaver's head. Since beaver were quite abundant in this area at that time, and since the tribe was accustomed to seeing and hunting them here, it was a logical identification. Today, a more active imagination is necessary to recognize the resemblance.

7. When a girl child was born, it was common for an elder woman in her clan to give her a symbol of the valuable work the child would contribute to her family and tribe throughout her life–a child-sized, root-digging stick. As a little girl, she would use this smaller version to imitate the work she saw the older women perform. When she attained full adulthood, the young woman would receive another digging stick; this digging stick, and subsequent others, were used throughout her married life and sometimes passed down to others in her family.

Typically, the digging stick's shaft was made from a straight-grained wood, cut or ground to an end-point, then repeatedly greased and charred in a slow fire to make it rock-hard. A notch at the top accommodated a cross-piece handle that could be made of horn, bone, or other wood. With the increased availability of iron and other metals for tool making, the wooden shafts were eventually replaced with the stronger materials. Camas, biscuit root, bitterroot,

and wild onion were a few of the edible roots and bulbs regularly gathered by Shoshoni women.

8. Today, the Three Forks referred to by Sacagawea is near the city of the same name in western Montana, between Butte and Bozeman. The rivers Lewis and Clark named "Jefferson," "Madison," and "Gallatin" still come together here in an exuberant expanse of water, wildlife, abundant vegetation, and protected topography. All of these factors had made the confluence a logical, long-term campsite for the Shoshone. The Jefferson River was named after President Thomas Jefferson; the Madison, after Secretary of State James Madison; and the Gallatin, after Albert Gallatin, Secretary of the Treasury. To the east of Three Forks, in what we today call the Bridger Range, the highest peak is known locally as Sacajawea Peak. This name was not bestowed by the Lewis and Clark Expedition, but came much later.

9. According to oral tradition, the Minnetaree had made a regular practice of raiding to obtain captives since the beginning of memory. With the introduction of the horse, their raids ran farther and farther afield, typically in the direction of the Rocky Mountains. In addition to providing an increased work force within the tribe–because captives were adopted, married, or otherwise assimilated into the various clans–these raids also increased the size of family units. For this reason, teenaged girls and girl children were especially desirable raid targets. Adult men and women, young men and older boys were not. The practice of raiding was certainly not unique to the Minnetaree, but in their willingness to adopt captives into their families, they were more generous than most.

10. Scholars estimate that roughly three to four thousand Mandan and Minnetaree lived along the Missouri at its juncture with the Knife when Sacagawea lived there.

An established commerce and trading center, this area was divided into five associated villages along a nine-mile stretch of the river that served as a marketing hub for the far-ranging Plains peoples. It was a true, multicultural crossroads that attracted traders from as far away as the American southwest and mid-eastern Canada.

11. Corn, beans, and squash are still widely known as "the three sisters," each dependent upon the other for optimal growth within the same planting. Other vegetables and sunflowers were sometimes grown along with these main three. Planting, tending, harvesting, and preparing the gardens' bounty was the work of women. Their gardening tools were prized symbols of the cyclical cultivation and abundance that gave this culture its stability. The gardens, tools, and produce belonged, officially, to the women, as did the villages' household goods and lodges. Men owned their weapons, pipes, and male horses.

12. The Shoshone were a highly mobile people. The demanding, often unforgiving lands they called home forced them to live frugally and attentively, to travel with a minimum of baggage, and to become experts at survival. The unpredictable availability of raw resources for food, clothing, and shelter did not allow for the sense of security that seemed commonplace to the Mandan and Minnetaree. To a girl Sacagawea's age, the material abundance and physical stability of her new life–the Minnetaree were called "Big Bellies" because their stomachs were always full–must have seemed a marked contrast to the stream-lined, sometimes harsh, lifestyle she had known with her birth people.

13. In addition to the many tribes that considered the Mandan enclave a principal trading hub, full- and part-time traders from companies sponsored by the French and British were regular visitors here. The North West Company and the Hudson's Bay Company were familiar names; Charbonneau himself had been a North West Company man. In this land, now known to Lewis and Clark as the Louisiana Purchase, the Mandan had been trading with the French since the early 1700s. Independents, or free traders, routinely brought their wares to the associated villages. Often they married into the tribes and maintained families there, while traveling seasonally to trap and trade.

14. The security of sizeable settlements in this land of abundant resources afforded the Minnetaree and their relatives a decided advantage. Established alliances between regionally- or linguistically-related tribes strengthened the villages by creating a power base against outside enemies, as well as providing a more diverse gene pool to make the tribes strong.

15. Sacagawea's mother would have begun training her daughter in the arts of survival when the child was about three years old. Throughout her life, Sacagawea would have been expected to accomplish demanding, unrelenting work, and accomplish it skillfully, respectfully, and without complaint. Her traditional Shoshoni work ethic may have seemed exceptional, even to the industrious Minnetaree. The Shoshone were, and still are, an ingenious and resourceful people.

The blue beads given to Sacagawea in her woman's belt–probably the type described by Lewis as *tiacommachuck* (chief beads)–were highly prized. They carried the mark of considerable distinction. The belt itself was a gift of honor. A woman could neither trade for, nor make one for herself; no direct blood relative could give her one. The belt had to come from the other women of the clan. That an adoptive member would be given this honor, speaks highly of Sacagawea's early training and her personal character. (See Bower's *Hidatsa Social and Ceremonial Organization*.)

16. Toussaint Charbonneau was a French Canadian/Métis trapper who had lived among native peoples for at least a decade, the last five years of which had been spent among the Minnetaree (Hidatsa). It is interesting to note that, apparently, these native peoples did not consider trappers/traders like Charbonneau to be white men in the same sense they did Lewis, Clark, and others of the Corps of Discovery. That designation seems to have been saved for those who did not become relatives among them.

17. That Toussaint Charbonneau had at least two Snake wives living with him at the Second Village, we know from the journals of Lewis and Clark. Oral tradition holds that the Hidatsa name for the first of these two wives meant "Otter Woman," and that she and Charbonneau already had a son Toussaint when Sacagawea appeared on the scene. This goes against popular belief that the additional Snake wife mentioned in the journals was a young Shoshoni girl who had been captured the same time as Sacagawea. Toussaint Charbonneau (Jr.) surfaces again in the personal papers of William Clark, some years after the Expedition. There, he is listed as having been under the care of Clark along with Sacagawea's two children, Jean Baptiste (Pomp) and Lizette Charbonneau. (See Jackson's *Letters of the Lewis and Clark Expedition.*)

18. Smoking of the pipe, in this sense, was a ceremonial event. In presentation of the pipe, different tribes had distinctive formalities associated with specific purposes. Men treasured their individual pipes, often decorating them with elaborate, sometimes symbolic, ornamentation. Some pipes might be kept in reverential reserve, to be used for only the most sacred or serious circumstances. Others might be smoked every day.

19. Construction of Fort Mandan began November 2, 1804, with the men felling large cottonwood, elm, and some ash, then rough-hewing the heavy logs and dragging them into position for placement. The weather worsened. Stones had to be gathered from the ice-rimmed river to build fireplaces. Mud and manure daubing to plug spaces between the logs was carried out in plummeting temperatures and blowing snow with nearly frozen fingers. The captains' quarters were finished first. Lewis and Clark moved in on November 20. The rest of the men continued to cover the V-shaped wings of joined rooms with ceiling puncheons, or flat-hewn logs. Their work did not end when darkness fell. Instead, they toiled into the wee morning hours for days, trying to keep ahead of the worsening weather. Finally, the gate was erected across the front of the structure, closing the V-shape into a triangle. A lookout tower and palisade (or wall) of sharpened logs completed the project. Temperatures plummeted into the sub-zero range and stayed there. A typical Dakota winter had begun.

20. Lewis's huge, Newfoundland dog unofficially joined the Corps of Discovery before most of the men. While on a trip to arrange for Expedition supplies, Lewis paid twenty dollars for him (a high price in those days). Why the captain suddenly felt compelled to have a canine companion, we don't know. Lewis's journals, however, do indicate a deep affection and high esteem for the dog. Seaman (sometimes misread in early translations as "Scannon") earned his keep on the Expedition by guarding the camp, hunting and retrieving game, and no doubt providing comic relief with his antics. A typical Newfoundland dog stands about two feet tall and can weigh as much as the average man. This breed is capable of strenuous labor, though no mention is made of such activity in the Expedition journals. It is recorded that Seaman consistently caused quite a stir among the many tribes with

whom he came into contact. No doubt their dogs were very different from this rollicking behemoth.

21. The term "Medicine" is sometimes used as verbal shorthand to describe that force of heart, spirit, or power that elevates a thing beyond its everyday existence. Medicine can be intensely private, or it can be shared and transmitted to others. Most native cultures worldwide share this concept, though their terms for it vary.

Physical contact (including sexual contact) was one of the primary methods of transferring Medicine. Sometimes this transferral was ritualized, sometimes not. Lewis's and Clark's many references to what they perceived as sexual promiscuity amongst the tribes had far more to do with transferral of Medicine than with loose morals.

22. This was the official primary objective of the Expedition. President Jefferson had charged Lewis and Clark with the location and mapping of the long-hoped-for Northwest Passage, whereby a water route across the continent would open up shipping and travel "from sea to shining sea." Not only would this provide the twenty-year-old nation with a commercial coup, but politically this would help cement the United States's claim on the lands and resources of the far West. At the time the Expedition was sent forth, many nations were jockeying for legal claim to these new lands; however, none of them seemed overly concerned with the sovereign rights of those peoples who, for generations, had called these lands home.

23. It is a fact that no one knew how long the Expedition might take. Trapper/trader Charbonneau was most likely a regular absentee from his family during prime hunting and trading months; he seems to have been a wanderer at heart, well suited to his chosen lifestyle. But, even he could not have foreseen that this particular journey would take him,

Sacagawea, and Pomp away from home for a year and four months, or that they would travel some five thousand miles before they saw the Mandan villages again. The Corps of Discovery traveled an additional year from their departure point in St. Louis, covering a total of some eight thousand miles on the Expedition. They were gone so long many thought they had died en route, and were shocked when the boats finally returned to home port.

24. Horses had come gradually to the Shoshone from descendants of the Spanish stock introduced by conquistadors into Mexico in the early 1500s. By the early 1700s, the horse was drastically changing centuries-old patterns of tribal life. Divisions between those people who had the horse and those who did not grew ever wider and more distinct. The material and cultural lives of the Mountain and Plains Shoshone became markedly different from those of the Great Basin Shoshone, who did not accept the horse. Sacagawea's birth people were Mountain Shoshone.

"The Shining Mountains" refer to what today are called the Rocky Mountains (which include many individual ranges such as the Bitterroots). In Lewis's estimation, "shining" described the nearly ever-present snow that blanketed the highest elevations.

25. This is a plausible explanation as to why Charbonneau's other Snake wife was not selected to accompany the Expedition as interpreter. Surely, if her birth people were of the same group as Sacagawea's, Otter Woman would have been the more logical choice. Her son, Toussaint, was not an infant at the time of the Expedition; he would have required less care during the journey, or could have remained in the care of Sacagawea and the Minnetaree relatives if his mother had been chosen to go. Sacagawea, on the other hand, was heavily pregnant at the time the choice was made, and, by the time the Expedition departed, carried a

nursing infant. The presence of a childless woman traveling with a party of men was no less a sign of friendly intent than a woman with an infant. Since Otter Woman–who seems to have been the logical choice–was not chosen, we must wonder why.

26. See endnote 16. Oral tradition tells us when the Agui Dika first saw the white men of the Corps of Discovery, they described them as having "faces paler than ashes," even though the men had been constantly sun- and wind-burned for over a year. In his journal entry dated August 13, 1805, Lewis notes that he rolled up his sleeve upon first meeting the Agui Dika to prove he was a white man. It seems he considered his face and hands to be "quite as dark as their own," an opinion apparently not shared by the tribe.

It is interesting to note Clark's description of October 29, 1804, in which he tells of a prairie fire in the Mandan Villages. His entry describes how "a boy, half white, was saved unhurt" by his (native) mother's quick thinking. The full passage goes on to say that the tribes credited the boy's survival not to his mother, but to "the boy's being white," and that his skin color was considered Big Medicine.

27. The typical translation chain for the Shoshoni language was: First, the English words were communicated by Lewis or Clark to interpreter François LaBiche, who spoke both English and French. LaBiche then translated into French for Charbonneau, who spoke French and Minnetaree (Hidatsa). Charbonneau spoke the words in Hidatsa to Sacagawea, who then translated them into Shoshoni. Any corresponding native responses went through the same process in reverse. This multi-staged communication technique was common not only with non-natives, but also at mass gatherings of multiple tribes where many "tongues" were spoken. The spoken word was often accompanied by, or substituted with, hand signals. These hand signs eventu-

ally amalgamated into a separate and distinct sign language, providing a quick, easy communication method commonly understood by many tribes and travelers.

28. Both Lewis and Clark had been doctoring the native peoples on the journey thus far. In most cases, this amounted to rudimentary care that fell under any physician's prime directive to first, do no harm. Some later cases required a surgeon's skill, however, such as amputation of frost-bitten toes and fingers. The captains' skills grew as the journey progressed. Lewis had made a point–after his personal tutorial by the eminent Dr. Benjamin Rush–of accumulating a hefty supply of medicines for the trip. These medicines included effective stop-gaps, soothers, and cures for ailments typical to soldiers on the march. Obviously, childbirth was one category that escaped his consideration.

Lewis's mother was widely regarded as an effective herbalist. Many women of her day relied upon home-grown remedies to doctor their families. It is likely both Lewis and Clark had grown up using all manner of organics as medicines. Of course, so had the native peoples. It was the white men's boxed pills, tinned powders, and bottled essential oils that caused so much excitement among the tribes. But these, too, had their limitations. The grave of Sergeant Floyd was testament to that.

29. René Jussome was another French-speaking trader/ interpreter who had married into the Mandan tribe. He and his family lived in the associated villages, and seem to have been friends with Charbonneau. Apparently, Jussome's wife and Sacagawea were at least nodding acquaintances, as they came together while the fort was still under construction to present gifts of buffalo robes to the officers. (See Howard's *Sacajawea* and Moulton's *Journals of John Ordway*.) When Charbonneau presented himself to Lewis and Clark on

November 4, 1804, Jussome had already been hired as an interpreter at the camp. Perhaps Jussome is the interpreter Charbonneau made a point of talking to before making his bid for employment. Though Lewis records his skepticism of Jussome's powdered snake rattle, Sacagawea probably had the opposite opinion after her son was born.

30. Some sources say the name Jean Baptiste was chosen by Charbonneau to honor a trader/trapper friend of his; it was a common name at that time. The Charbonneau family, however, points out that Jean Baptiste was the name of Toussaint Charbonneau's father. It is logical that he would follow tradition to name his second son after his father, since he had named his first son (by Otter Woman) after himself.

31. Included in the goods carried on the Expedition was *The Experiment*, a collapsible boat designed by Lewis for easier portages. *The Experiment* was actually the iron framework of a boat, fabricated at great expense and delay, specifically for this expedition. Originally, Lewis's idea was to cover the "ribs" of the boat with tree bark as the native peoples did in the East. But when *The Experiment* was called into use, there weren't enough suitable trees to cover it. Lewis then decided to encase the boat in leather, sewing the hides together and sealing the seams with grease and pitch. It seemed a feasible idea on dry land, but when the leather got wet, the seams stretched and gapped. The sealant wouldn't hold; the boat leaked like a sieve; and, when the leather dried, the hides shrank. The *Experiment* lived up to its name, and no amount of ingenious tinkering along the route could make it a success. After months of frustration with the boat's failings, Lewis finally ordered it sunk, and bid "Lewis'[s] Folly" good riddance.

32. The Corps of Discovery had a wide variety of arms also packed in and on the boats at Ft. Mandan. This included muskets, rifles, espontoons (spear-headed braces against which rifles could be steadied) and bayonets, pistols, knives, swords, tomahawks, and (war) axes. An air gun, a swivel cannon, and a pair of blunderbusses rounded out the arsenal.

33. Perhaps the most attractive feature of placing a child in a cradleboard was that of immobility. The arms were wrapped close to the body and the legs bundled together. Only the head was free to move from side to side. Thus cocooned, the child was supported upright by the cradleboard frame and protected against accidents that came from sudden or erratic movement. It was possible to stand, lay, or prop the cradleboard away from the mother, leaving her free to work without the worry of watching her baby's every movement. The cradleboard could also be carried on the mother's back, supported by a chest or head strap. The word "cradleboard" does not appear in the Expedition journals, only the word *hier*, which has been interpreted to mean a proper cradleboard. It is still common, however, for women from many cultural backgrounds to carry their infants and young children in a sling of cloth on their backs, or balanced on their hips. It is plausible that Sacagawea used this method, too.

34. The flattish pirogues and large keelboat were stable river craft in the hands of an experienced boatman, but Charbonneau—like most people who cannot swim—had a penchant for panic on the water. As a trapper, he may have had experience with canoes, but apparently did not have much skill with other types of craft such as the pirogue he was piloting this day. The boats were pushed, cordelled (pulled) with a rope, long-poled, rowed, or sailed on the river. Sometimes they were portaged (carried or dragged) on the river bank. The Expedition struggled constantly against the current until they reached the Continental Divide.

Unseen treacheries of submerged snags, boulders, and sand-bars were only worsened by unpredictable wind gusts, making any day on the river anything but relaxing.

35. The tradition of giving medallions to important tribal chiefs was established in this country by the Spanish, French, and British, who made the first contacts with native peoples. In this, they were carrying out a centuries-old tradition that called for an exchange of gifts of state between high ranking visitors and local rulers. It was common for medallions or medals to bear the likeness of the visitors' head of state. The Corps of Discovery's inventory rosters show medals of five sizes. Some bore Jefferson's profile; others, figures from George Washington's administration. Some were silver, some bronze, and some medals may have merely been US coins with a ring attached, or a hole bored into them to accommodate a neck ribbon.

36. President Jefferson had ordered both Lewis and Clark to keep a log of their observations along the route. This included latitudinal and longitudinal readings, weather information, and other scientific data in categories such as geology, botany, biology, and zoology. In addition, data that would now be covered by the disciplines of cultural anthropology, paleontology, cartography, linguistics, and more, would have been required. The captains, in turn, charged some of their men with keeping journals. Unfortunately, this particular order seems to have been regarded by the men as just one more in a long list of chores. Their records, on the whole, do not display the depth or variety of detail seen in the journals of either Lewis or Clark; they are often perfunctory, almost terse; one can almost hear the men grumbling as they try to piece together the day's events.

37. "Buffalo Jump" is somewhat of a misnomer since the animals did not willingly jump over the bluffs, but were stampeded from behind. It was a most effective, food-gathering technique for the natives. For the buffalo however, the result was a grotesque and, often, lingering death. They fell one upon another in piles so deep, many suffocated before they could die from their injuries. The stench was beyond description, especially in late summer when temperatures soared. Even so, the abundance of meat and hides these jumps produced fed the tribes well, and ensured their survival through the long winters. Wildlife scavengers, too, grew to depend upon these windfalls of food.

38. It is recorded in the journals that Sacagawea grew sick earlier, as well. Mostly, her illnesses seem to have been fevers, which is not surprising for a first-time, breast-feeding mother who daily had to sustain the rigorous, physical output this journey demanded. Modern historians also conjecture that her recurring symptoms may indicate chronic pelvic inflammatory disease. This particular illness, whatever its source, proved serious. She nearly died. What would happen to Pomp? How would the Corps communicate with the Shoshones for the required and essential horses? And what of the peaceful intent symbolized by a woman traveling with a party of men? The captains knew that without Sacagawea's connection with the Shoshones, the Expedition's odds of making it over and through the Shining Mountains successfully were slim. The mission was in jeopardy.
Note: The Time of the Long Grass is the traditional reference to the midsummer season.

39. The scientific name of this plant is *Psoralea esculenta*. In true scientific form, Lewis collected a sample that survived the Expedition and is now at the Academy of Natural Sciences in Philadelphia. Many of the plant specimens collected during the journey did not survive. The caches were infiltrated by winter/spring runoff, ground seep, and flood

waters that ruined the often irreplaceable stored goods. Only about two hundred pressed and dried plant specimens collected by Lewis and Clark made their way back to "the U. States." Although there is some argument as to the exact number, scholars credit the explorers with the discovery of eighty to one hundred and twenty plant species previously unknown to the scientific community.

The "prairie apple" was, and is, sometimes also called "white apple" or "breadroot." The Plains tribes made wide use of its bulb, which could been eaten raw or boiled like today's potatoes. Bulbs were commonly dug from late summer until first frost, strung together to dry in the sun, then stored whole, or pulverized into chunks or powder. After eating so little for days while she was sick, Sacagawea shocked her weakened digestive system with the feast of unripe prairie apples. Her body rebelled. She relapsed, and her fever returned.

40. Sergeant Gass's journals state that the hailstones were seven inches in circumference. This is not at all unusual for severe prairie storms in late spring or early summer. Forty years later, emigrants in covered wagons would record hailstones the size of hen's eggs in these violent storms, and say the hail "brained" oxen dead as they stood unprotected in the open. Often, the ground would be drifted over with hailstones, as if by a winter storm with blowing snow. Today, the sheer force of such pounding hail storms flattens crops, breaks windows, and dents car bodies.

41. Clark writes that all of Pomp's clothes were lost. Presumably they were in, or attached to, the cradleboard. A compass, Clark's *fusee* (aka fusil or officer's musket), and his umbrella were also swept away in the gully washer. Perhaps Clark had opened the umbrella in the ravine to help shield the group from the rain, only to have it jerked from his hand by the fierce winds or the sudden, churning waters of the flash

flood. The compass was retrieved the next day, found in the mud and stones at the mouth of the now empty ravine. This was a true stroke of luck, as the compass was vitally important. Clark's musket and umbrella were never recovered.

42. It is not clear why Lewis decided to leave Charbonneau and Sacagawea behind; it does not seem to have been a logical choice. Lewis's mounting frustration and impatience may have clouded his judgment. If there was a compelling reason for leaving Sacagawea behind with Clark and the others, we do not find it in the journals. Indeed, since Lewis knew that the presence of a woman traveling in a group of men signaled peaceful intent, his departure without her seems to make no sense at all. Everything worked out well in the end, but by taking Sacagawea with him, Lewis could have avoided the confusion that occurred when he first encountered the Shoshone.

43. The Shoshoni word for stranger, or "one apart," is currently spelled as stated in the text. Lewis apparently heard the letter "v" as a "b" when it was spoken by Sacagawea to Charbonneau, so he said something like *tabbabone* when he tried to speak to the tribeswomen. Tabbabone is how Lewis recorded the word in his journal.

44. The substance Lewis used to paint the women's faces was vermillion. Technically, vermillion is a bright red mercuric sulfide, though the term has also been used to describe a variety of reddish-colored earths. Vermillion was favored by the tribes as pigment to color skin, hides, and hair. Like many other earth-based materials, it was ground or pounded into powder, then mixed with fat, saliva, and natural plant juices (or sometimes blood) to form a spreadable paste. The brilliant color was commonly applied in patterns with the fingers to denote beauty, status, or—in this case—peace.

Lewis laid in a considerable supply of vermillion for the Expedition to trade with the tribes, as it was already in great demand.

45. The way this is recorded in the journals, Cameahwait is represented as Sacagawea's brother, which, to the captains, meant that he and she shared the same parents by physical birth. But, the Shoshone had a less restricted definition of the term; there are many levels of kinship within the tribe that do not have direct equivalents in non-native society. Cameahwait may have been a clan brother–that is, of Sacagawea's clan, but not necessarily progeny of the same parents. Regardless of their genetic relationship, the chance reunion of Sacagawea and her brother fits the adage that truth is, indeed, stranger than fiction.

46. This, again, shows the latitude of relationship within the clan. On the day Sacagawea adopted her nephew Bazil (or Shoogan), he became her son, not her nephew; she became his mother, not his aunt. Thereafter, Sacagawea had an additional name among her people, "Mother of Bazil." It appears that Bazil remained with Cameahwait's band when Sacagawea and the others continued west.

47. As it turned out, the return route of the Expedition in 1806 did not include another encounter with Sacagawea's people. Clark, Charbonneau, and Sacagawea went south and east along the Yellowstone River, effectively skirting the traditional summering grounds of the Shoshone.

48. Parched corn had been purchased from the Mandan the previous spring. It traveled well. Thrown into broth or water, it became tender; pounded into a powder, it could thicken soups; combined with grease or fat, it could be pressed into edible "cakes." It could also be baked into bread, or boiled into gruel. Cameahwait said that, of all the food gifts presented to him by his sister, he liked parched corn and sugar the best. Sacagawea undoubtedly knew many ways to prepare the parched corn, as Mandan and Minnetaree women prided themselves on their ability to help feed The People. Lewis remarked in his journal about the din of women pounding corn in the villages. He said the incessant pounding reminded him of a nail factory.

49. Scholarly opinion is divided as to the nature of "carry-soup" (or portable soup)–all 193 pounds of it listed on the Expedition roster. Was it the equivalent of today's instant, powdered, or dehydrated soup? Or was it more gelatinous, a thick, sticky concentrate that had to be poured or ladled? Military manuals of the day describe a concoction that was boiled down from various meats to a congealed paste, cut and baked until hard, then sealed in jars or tins. This would seem to be similar to today's bouillon cubes. Exactly what was contained in Lewis's portable soup canisters cannot be said with certainty. It is known that the portable soup was highly valued as an emergency ration, and that it served as a base for many a night's meal when game grew scarce. At one point–between leaving the Shoshone camp and making contact with the Nez Perce–Lewis listed twenty pounds of grease candles as a food supplement to the portable soup. (See Chuinard's *Only One Man Died.*)

50. Modern scholars maintain that Lewis obtained a number of colts specifically to supplement what he knew would be a bleak diet. It was not unheard of as a survival tactic in military campaigns of the time to eat horse meat. However, this story is being told from Sacagawea's viewpoint, and the idea of eating either horse or dog was shocking and abhorrent to her.

According to his notes, Clark never developed a taste for dog meat either. He seemed to view eating it as strictly a necessity. Lewis, on the other hand, became quite fond of the taste, saying he thought it as good as any meat and better than some. That Sacagawea kept up her strength without the nourishment of this meat, and still successfully nursed Pomp, is a testimony to the physical fortitude and mental toughness that were typical of her tribal upbringing.

51. Tribal tradition holds that the old woman Wetkuiis (roughly translated, the name means "that which was lost, then found") spoke so forcefully for the lives of these strangers that their lives were saved. As the Corps was near desperation at this time, it is questionable whether they would have survived without the Nez Perce's generosity. It is said Wetkuiis died only days after the white men appeared.

52. The journals record that these people were also called the Chopunnish. Typically, native tribes were known by a variety of names, though in their own languages they usually referred to themselves as The People or some similar term. The other names often originated with outside groups or tribes and identified some distinctive feature or socio/political status that would quickly and accurately be understood. Nez Perce, for instance, means "pierced nose" in French; Anasazi means "enemy" in Navajo. It is easy to see how this multitude of identities could lead to misconceptions and false impressions within non-native society. Thomas Jefferson, for instance, was convinced there was a lost nation of "Welsh Indians" in the far West, and was eager for Lewis and Clark to find them.

53. Twisted Hair, or Walammottinin, had a remarkable way of wearing his hair, even among his own people whose men were noted for their distinctive hair styles. His name means, more precisely, "forelock bundled and tied," which differs from the high, wide cockscomb of hair that typically rose from the men's foreheads in this tribe. This shock of hair was often held stiffly aloft with a saturation of animal fat mixed with pulverized earth. Sometimes the mineral

dust was colored. This style gave the men the appearance of being even taller than they were and added to their already proud bearing. Perhaps Walammottinin wore his hair more in the style of many Plains medicine men of that time. Karl Bodmer, in his paintings twenty-five years after the Lewis and Clark Expedition, recorded forelock bundles among men of spiritual standing.

54. The time of year the Expedition traveled down the Columbia is important in realizing why the tribes did not want to sell their "good" salmon. Winter was coming. This was the time of preparing and laying by of foods that would ensure the tribes' survival through the next spring. Salmon swim upriver only seasonally and are not the limitless source of food the captains may have assumed they were. The journals comment on the overwhelming stench of the fish being prepared for winter, along the Columbia. There was smoked fish, dried fish, boiled fish, and pounded fish, as well. The tribes cannot be faulted for their survival instinct; they knew what a long, Pacific Northwest winter was like. The captains did not.

55. The discovery of tribes who obviously had extensive experience with white traders seems to have been met with a mixture of surprise, consternation, and an element of (temporary) relief. If ships plied the coast with trade goods, Lewis reasoned they might also carry supplies that he could appropriate, or at least acquire on credit with his papers from President Jefferson. This did not come to pass. Also, rumors of white settlers on the coast proved disappointing. The bottom line seems to have been that the tribes were quick studies when it came to trading with the whites. They knew the value of their own goods and knew Lewis's and Clark's need to trade would work to the tribes' advantage. Eventually, the Corps was reduced to cutting the buttons off their uniform coats to help sweeten the deal when their trade goods were all but exhausted.

It should also be noted, however, that there were numerous recorded instances of tribesmen bringing gifts of food to the Corps during the long winter, with no apparent expectation of trade or purchase.

56. It is not recorded whether Sacagawea offered her belt of blue beads, or whether it was traded away without her consent. It seems unlikely that she would have willingly parted with something so dear, especially for a luxury item such as the sea otter robe Lewis coveted. The journals say that the Chinooks specifically named the blue (or "chief") beads as the item they would accept in exchange for the otter skin robe.

57. This is the much-touted vote that puts Sacagawea and York into a classification all their own in American politics. The Corps of Discovery was a formal military expedition into the great unknown, initiated by the President and funded by Congress. As such, it carried the legal sovereignty of the United States with it. In essence, wherever the Corps was, there was the United States also, at least in the mind of the American government. So technically–although a bit of a stretch to modern minds–this vote took place in America.

How much formality there was to the vote is unknown. It was possibly just an individual voicing of opinion. Sacagawea, practical as ever, cast her vote for the location where there would be plenty of *wappato*, or *pota*, roots to eat. She was outvoted. Still, it remains an extraordinary event.

Had this group been in Philadelphia or any other, so-called, civilized American city of the day, the opportunity to participate in a formal decision–let alone, to vote–would not have been afforded a woman, nor a slave. That Sacagawea as a native woman was asked for her vote by these non-natives was extraordinary for its time. That York, as a black slave, was given an equal vote with his master and other free men, was simply unheard of in polite American society. The wilderness was the great equalizer.

58. Those at Fort Clatsop became aware of the beached whale when two of the Corpsmen who had been tending the saltworks were given a considerable amount of whale blubber by some Clatsop and Tillamook families living nearby. After cooking it, the men pronounced it similar in taste to beaver, and a welcome change from the lean elk they were so tired of eating.

59. Though he is not mentioned specifically in the journals as being at this site, it is safe to assume that Pomp (not yet a year old) was there with his mother and father, rather than being left behind at the fort.

60. Out of the entire four and a half months spent at Fort Clatsop, only twelve days were without rain; even fewer had any appreciable sunshine. Scholars today speculate about the influences of El Niño and La Niña on weather excesses, and debate whether the winter of 1805-6 could have been the result of those kind of patterns. That winter, all clothing supplies and foodstuffs were recorded as being sodden, flea-ridden, dark, and dank. If ever there existed a recipe for clinical depression, Fort Clatsop had every ingredient that year.

61. These caches were typical deep storage pits dug into hillsides or other protected areas, where chances of remaining undisturbed were greatest. Typically, they were lined with rocks, branches, and other leafy organics. Once filled with the goods being cached, the original soil from the hole was shoveled on top to seal it. The ground surface was then restored to as close to pristine as possible, in hopes no one would detect the disturbance. Everything–from foodstuffs to tobacco, pelts to muskets, and clothing to scientific specimens–was secreted in this way, with the intent that the Corps would retrieve them on the return trip. The storage method was unreliable; in one breached cache alone, Lewis lost the entire collection of plants he had assembled between

Fort Mandan and the Great Falls. Groundwater had proven to be a more effective enemy than man.

62. On July 3, 1806, Lewis and his group of men rode on horseback to the Sun River country and White Bear Islands in present-day Montana, then north to explore the Marias River. Clark took the rest of the men, York, Sacagawea, Charbonneau, and Pomp, along with the remainder of the horses, and headed down the Yellowstone River.

63. This is what is known today as Pompey's Pillar, just outside present-day Billings, Montana. Long before Clark arrived, the Crow Nation called it "Where the Mountain Lion Lies," and it carried considerable importance in Crow culture. The rock form consists of sandstone, scientifically known as Hell Creek sandstone. Like a giant fist, it rises from the banks of the Yellowstone River, providing a spectacular view of the surrounding lowlands and river bluffs. Today, this site sports the only remaining physical/geographical evidence from the Lewis and Clark Expedition. William Clark's carved signature can be plainly seen from the visitor walkway at this national historic landmark.

64. There has been some speculation that Pompey's Tower was named after the Roman general who was a contemporary of Julius Caesar. It seems far more likely, however, that it was named primarily for Sacagawea's Pomp, the good-natured "dancing boy" with whom Clark had shared camp for almost a year and a half. It is clear from his post-Expedition correspondence and personal legal papers that Clark had a genuine affection for the little boy. He offered to adopt Pomp at the end of Charbonneau's employment, and some years later was named the boy's legal guardian.

In his Virginia upbringing during the Age of Enlightenment, Clark would have been exposed to the classic names of ancient Greek and Roman literature. It was even commonplace in Clark's day to attach such names to slaves in the American South. Perhaps Clark was reminded of General Pompey when he heard Pomp's name spoken. Perhaps he thought the longer name sounded more grand, more fitting for such a remarkable rock. Or perhaps, because Pompey was a familiar name and the Shoshoni version had no particular meaning to him, Clark had called Pomp Pompey all along. The journals do not enlighten us on this point.

65. A few academic sources explore the possibility that Cruzatte knew his target was Captain Lewis, and shot anyway. Tempers were very short by this time. Disagreements and battles of will were common. It was known that Cruzatte and Lewis quarreled; in that, the fiddler was not alone. The Lewis of the return trip was not the same Lewis who had left the Mandan villages for the Pacific Ocean, if the tone of his journal entries are any indication. He seems more strident and agitated, quicker to respond with anger and to place blame, more prone to jump into the thick of things when a cooler head would have served him better. He seems far more prone to self-doubt. Lewis had been known to suffer from "melancholia" since his boyhood. Modern medical experts now wonder if the symptoms intimated by his journal entries indicate episodes of chronic clinical depression. He was not easy to live with, but then, driven men rarely are.

In Cruzatte's defense, any leather-clad, wind-whipped, sun-burned, and largely camouflaged (by foliage) target could have easily been mistaken for an elk. Especially when the hunter only had one eye, as Cruzatte did, and a near-sighted one at that!
Note: The Time of the Berry Moon refers to late summer.

66. Clark later wrote a letter to Charbonneau, commended him for his service on the Expedition, and offered to help set him up in the future should Charbonneau decide to try his

hand at civilization. He again expressed his appreciation for Sacagawea's participation and his desire to remain involved in the life of little Pomp. (Presumably, Charbonneau would have had to have someone translate the letter into French for him. It is not known whether Charbonneau could read.) According to Clark's account, Sacagawea was agreeable to his taking Pomp when the boy was older. We have no documentation from her to confirm or deny this. We do know from legal records that Pomp, Toussaint (Jr.), and Pomp's younger sister, Lizette, did travel to St. Louis some years later, and did come under the guardianship of Clark.

67. The word was out: a trapper's paradise lay to the west, along the route Lewis and Clark had just traveled. At the Mandan Village, the enterprising John Colter asked for–and received–a discharge from further duties with the Corps. He, and several other trappers, immediately turned their faces upriver and paddled back into the wilderness. A new era was underway. The life, the land, and the people Sacagawea had known would never again be the same.

Bibliography

Ackerman, Lillian A., ed. *A Song To The Creator: Traditional Arts of Native American Women of the Plateau.* Norman, OK, and London: University of Oklahoma Press, 1996.

Allen, Paula Gunn. *The Sacred Hoop: Recovering the Feminine in American Indian Traditions.* Boston: Beacon Press, 1986.

Ambrose, Stephen E. *Lewis & Clark: Voyage of Discovery.* Washington, DC: National Geographic Society, 1998.

_____. *Undaunted Courage.* New York: Simon & Schuster, 1996.

Anderson, Irving W. "Probing the Riddle of Bird Woman." *Montana: The Magazine of Western History* (October 1973): (n.p.).

_____. "Sacajawea? Sakakawea? Sacagawea?: Spelling, Pronunciation, Meaning." *We Proceeded On.* Lewis and Clark Trail Heritage Foundation Publication, (Summer 1975): (n.p.).

_____. *A Charbonneau Family Portrait.* Astoria, OR: Fort Clatsop Historical Association, 1988.

Bakeless, John. *Lewis and Clark: Partners in Discovery.* New York: William Morrow & Co., 1947.

_____, ed. *Journals of Lewis and Clark.* New York: Penguin Books, 1964.

Bergon, Frank, ed. *The Journals of Lewis and Clark.* New York: Penguin Books, 1989.

Biddle, Nicholas. *The Journals of the Expedition under the Command of Capts. Lewis and Clark.* 1814. Reprint, special 2 vol. edition, New York: Heritage Press, 1962.

Blevins, Winifred. *Charbonneau: Man of Two Dreams.* Ottawa, IL: Jameson Books, 1975.

Bowers, Alfred W. *Hidatsa Social and Ceremonial Organization.* Revision, Bulletin No. 194, Smithsonian Institution's Bureau of Ethnology. Lincoln, NE, and London: University of Nebraska Press, 1992.

Brown, Marion Marsh. *Sacagawea: Indian Interpreter to Lewis and Clark.* Chicago: Children's Press, 1988.

Burroughs, Raymond Darwin. *The Natural History of the Lewis and Clark Expedition.* East Lansing, MI: Michigan State University Press, 1995.

Catlin, George. *Letters and Notes on the Manners, Customs, and Conditions of the North American Indians.* 2 vols. 1844. Reprint, New York: Dover Publications, 1973.

_____. *Letters and Notes on the North American Indians.* Edited by Michael MacDonald. New York: Gramercy Books, 1975.

Clark, Ella E., and Margot Edmonds. *Sacagawea of the Lewis and Clark Expedition.* Berkeley, CA: University of California Press, 1979.

Chuinard, E.G. *Only One Man Died: The Medical Aspects of the Lewis and Clark Expedition.* 1979. Reprint, Fairfield, WA: Ye Galleon Press, 1997.

Cody, Iron Eyes. *Indian Talk: Hand Signals of the American Indian.* Healdsburg, CA: Naturegraph Co., 1970.

Crawford, Helen. "Sakakawea." *North Dakota Historical Quarterly.* (April 1927): (n.p.).

Crofts, Beatrice, and Elinor Markley. *Walk Softly, This Is God's Country.* Lander, WY: Mortimore Publishers, 1997.

Curtis, Natalie, ed. *The Indians' Book: Authentic Legends, Lore, and Music.* Avenel, NJ: Gramercy Books, 1987.

Cutbush, Edward. *Observations on the Means of Preserving the Health of Soldiers and Sailors.* Philadelphia, PA: Fry & Kannerer, 1808.

DeVoto, Bernard. *Across the Wide Missouri.* New York: Bonanza Books, 1957.

_____. *The Course of Empire.* Boston: Houghton Mifflin Co., 1952.

_____, ed. *The Journals of Lewis and Clark.* Boston: Houghton Mifflin Co., 1953.

Doane, Nancy Locke. *The Indian Doctor Book.* Charlotte, NC: Aerial Photography Services, Inc., 1985.

Dramer, Kim. *The Shoshone.* Philadelphia: Chelsea House Publishers, 1996.

Eastman, Charles Alexander. *Soul of the Indian.* Boston: Houghton Mifflin Co., 1980.

Fifer, Barbara, and Vicky Soderberg. *Along The Trail With Lewis And Clark.* Great Falls, MT: Montana Magazine Press, 1998.

Gilbert, Bill. *The Trail Blazers.* New York: Time Life Books, 1973.

Hebard, Grace Raymond. *Sacajawea: A Guide and Interpreter of the Lewis And Clark Expedition.* Glendale, CA: Arthur H. Clark Company, 1957.

Heinbuch, Jean. *A Quillwork Companion.* Liberty, UT: Eagle's View Publishing Co., 1990.

Hensler, Christy Ann. *Guide to Indian Quillworking.* Surrey, British Columbia: Hancock House, 1989.

Horner, John B. *Days and Deeds in the Oregon Country.* Portland, OR: JK Gill Co., 1928.

Howard, Ella Mae. *Lewis and Clark: Exploration of Central Montana.* Lewis and Clark Interpretive Assoc., 1993.

Howard, Harold P. *Sacajawea.* Norman, OK: University of Oklahoma Press, 1971.

Hungry Wolf, Adolph. *Traditional Dress.* Summertown, TN: Book Publishing Co., 1990.

Jackson, Donald, ed. *Letters of the Lewis and Clark Expedition with Related Documents, 1783-1854.* Urbana, IL: University of Illinois Press, 1962.

Johnson, Charles Grier Jr. *Common Plants of the Inland Pacific Northwest.* Washington, DC: USDA Forest Service, GPO, 1993.

Josephy, Alvin M. Jr. *The Nez Perce Indians and the Opening of the Northwest.* New Haven, CT: Yale University Press, 1965.

Kessler, Donna J. *The Making of Sacagawea: A Euro-American Legend.* Tuscaloosa, AL: University of Alabama Press, 1996.

Kroll, Steven. *Lewis and Clark: Explorers of the American West.* New York: Holiday House, 1994.

La Farge, Oliver. *Pictorial History of the American Indian.* New York: Crown Publishers, 1956.

Large, Arlen J. "Sacagawea Takes Her Place with the Goddess of Love and Beauty." *We Proceeded On.* Lewis and Clark Trail Heritage Foundation Publication (November 1989): (n.p.).

Madsen, Brigham. *The Lemhi: Sacajawea's People.* Caldwell, ID: Caxton Printers Ltd., 1979.

Moulton, Gary E., ed. *The Journals of the Lewis and Clark Expedition.* 8 vols. Lincoln, NE, and London: University of Nebraska Press, 1986-1993.

_____, ed. *The Journals of John Ordway and Charles Floyd.* Vol. 9. Lincoln, NE, and London: University of Nebraska Press, 1995.

_____, ed. *The Journal of Patrick Gass.* Vol. 10. Lincoln, NE, and London: University of Nebraska Press, 1996.

_____, ed. *The Journals of Joseph Whitehouse.* Vol. 11. Lincoln, NE, and London: University of Nebraska Press, 1997.

Murphy, Dan. *Lewis and Clark: Voyage of Discovery.* Las Vegas, NV: KC Publications, 1977.

Osgood, Ernest S., ed. *The Field Notes of Capt. William Clark, 1803-1805.* New Haven, CT: Yale University, 1964.

Paterek, Josephine. *Encyclopedia of American Indian Costume.* New York: WW Norton & Co., 1994.

Peebles, John J. *Lewis and Clark in Idaho.* Boise, ID: Idaho Historical Society, 1966.

Reid, Russell. *Sakakawea, The Bird Woman.* Bismarck, ND: State Historical Society of North Dakota, 1986.

Ronda, James P. *Lewis and Clark Among The Indians.* Lincoln, NE, and London: University of Nebraska Press, 1984.

_____, ed. *Voyages of Discovery: Essays on the Lewis and Clark Expedition.* Helena, MT: Montana State Historical Society Press, 1998.

Schroer, Blanche. "Boat Pusher or Bird Woman?" *Annals of Wyoming.* (Spring 1980): (n.p.).

Schultz, James Willard. *Bird Woman.* Boston and New York: Houghton Mifflin Co., 1918.

Seton, Ernest Thompson. *Sign Talk.* New York: Doubleday, Page, and Co., 1918.

Snyder, Gerald S. *In the Footsteps of Lewis and Clark.* Washington, DC: National Geographic Society, 1970.

Thomas, Davis, and Karen Ronnefeldt, eds. *People of the First Man: The Paintings of Karl Bodmer.* New York: Dutton, 1976.

Thomasma, Kenneth. *Naya Nuki: Shoshoni Girl Who Ran Away.* Grand Rapids, MI: Baker Book House, and Jackson, WY: Grandview Publishing, 1991.

_____. *The Truth About Sacajawea.* Jackson, WY: Grandview Publishing Company, 1997.

Thwaites, Reuben Gold, ed. *Original Journals of the Lewis and Clark Expedition, 1804-1806.* 8 vols. New York: Dodd, Mead, 1904-1905.

Walker, Deward E. Jr. *Indians of Idaho.* Moscow, ID: University of Idaho Press, 1978.

Wheeler, Olin D. *The Trail of Lewis and Clark, 1804-1904.* 2 vols. New York: G.P. Putnam's Sons, 1904.

Wilson, Gilbert. *Waheenee: An Indian Girl's Story told by herself to Gilbert L. Wilson, 1839.* 1921. Reprint, Lincoln NE, and London: University of Nebraska Press, 1981.

Native oral traditions concerning the historical person Sacagawea and her participation in the Lewis and Clark Expedition have also been consulted and given equal consideration in the creation of this work.

Spelling and Grammar

Spelling and grammar in the early 1800s were not the exact practices they are today. At that time, fewer people were able to read; far fewer could write. Captain Lewis, though educated personally by President Jefferson at Monticello, would have won no spelling bees. Captain Clark was even worse. Therefore, it is not surprising that throughout the written records of their journey, words do not always follow modern structure or rules. In the field journals, words (even proper names) are often spelled incompletely or incorrectly. Sometimes words are spelled one way in a certain entry, and a completely different way in another.

The tribal languages and French words and phrases unfamiliar to Lewis and Clark were spelled even more creatively. This is understandable. When traveling in an unfamiliar neighborhood, city, or country today, most of us will attempt to speak (and write) phonetically; we try to "sound things out." This is exactly what the members of the Corps of Discovery did. As a result, many of the journal entries are best understood when read aloud in the "sounding out" method, rather than relying strictly on the dictionary.

To make journal quotations and excerpts more reader-friendly, modern spellings, grammar, and punctuation have been used.

Quotations from the Journals

Bracketed words and phrases within the quotes have been inserted for clarity by the author. They may reflect information found in the editorial notes from the following transcriptions of the Lewis and Clark journals: Nicholas Biddle (1814); Reuben Thwaites (1904–5); John Bakeless (1964); Frank Bergon (1989); and Gary E. Moulton (1986–99). These editions, in their respective formats, represent the best scholarly research and interpretation of the journals to date.

The quotations should be read with a mind to the prevailing cultural orientations of their day. In dealing with history, we cannot accurately or fairly judge yesterday by today's standards. The best we can do is strive for a clear understanding of what happened, and why, in the appropriate context.

In addition, Lewis and Clark used the term "Minnetaree" to describe many related tribes of the region, including Hidatsa. The word is used in that context throughout the text.

Regarding Photographs and Illustrations

The intent with the photographs and illustrations used in this book is to give the reader a "sense" of what Sacagawea would have known in her daily life.

Most of the landscape photographs featured depict what is today north central Idaho and southwestern Montana. This was Sacagawea's homeland, the land of her birth and her annual travels between Summer Camps and Winter Camps. Today, much of this area is still wilderness, inaccessible to general automobile travel. Some of this wilderness burned in the wild fires of Summer/Fall, 2000.

The artifacts shown would have been familiar to Sacagawea and her contemporaries. When reproductions are pictured, this fact is noted in the captions.

Photo and Illustration Credits

Copyright is held by Organization, Photographer, or Illustrator unless otherwise noted.

Page

frvii Meadowlark
Original art by Joyce Badgley Hunsaker

2-3 Map
Courtesy of the Montana Historical Society, Helena, Montana

4 Banks of the Pack River, Selkirk Mountains, Idaho
Photography by Jay W. Krajic

6 Camas roots and bulbs
Courtesy of USDA Forest Service, Lewis and Clark National Historic Trail Interpretive Center, Great Falls

Basket
USDI/BLM National Historic Oregon Trail Interpretive Center, Baker City, Oregon

Root-digging stick
Courtesy of USDA Forest Service, Lewis and Clark National Historic Trail Interpretive Center, Great Falls

6-7 Little Camas Prairie, Idaho
Photography by Jay W. Krajic

8 Medicine Pouch, Quill Bracelet, Necklaces
Photography by Terry McGrew, McGrew Photography
© Joyce Badgley Hunsaker and Towanda, Inc.

Elkskin Shirt
Courtesy of USDA Forest Service, Lewis and Clark National Historic Trail Interpretive Center, Great Falls

9 Headwaters of Salmon River
Photography by Jay W. Krajic

10 Midday Sun
Courtesy of the National Museum of American Art, Smithsonian Institution. Gift of Mrs. Joseph Harrison, Jr.

11 Mandan Earth Lodge
Courtesy of the State Historical Society of North Dakota

Mandan Village
Courtesy of the National Museum of American Art, Smithsonian Institution. Gift of Mrs. Joseph Harrison, Jr.

12 Aspen
Photography by Jay W. Krajic

13 Pehriska Ruhpa
Courtesy of the State Historical Society of North Dakota

14 Bunchberry
Photography by Jay W. Krajic

15 Willow Fish Weir
Courtesy of USDA Forest Service, Lewis and Clark National Historic Trail Interpretive Center, Great Falls

16 Black Moccasin
Courtesy of the National Museum of American Art, Smithsonian Institution. Gift of Mrs. Joseph Harrison, Jr.

Fort Mandan
Courtesy of the North Dakota Lewis and Clark Interpretive Center

17 Thomas Jefferson's Medicine Chest
    Courtesy of Monticello and Thomas Jefferson
    Memorial Foundation. By kind permission
    of Mrs. Prentice Cooper.

18 Mandan Dog Sled
    Courtesy of the State Historical Society of
    North Dakota

19 Antelope, Prairie Dog
    Photography by J. Nevin Thompson

    Cradleboard
    Photography by Author

20 Knife and Sheath
    Photography by Terry McGrew, McGrew Photography
    © Joyce Badgley Hunsaker and Towanda, Inc.

21 Glacial Plain
    Photography by Jay W. Krajic

22 Peace Medal
    Photography by Terry McGrew, McGrew Photography
    © Joyce Badgley Hunsaker and Towanda, Inc.

    Chief of the Blood Indians, Vignette, Tableau 46
    Courtesy of the Joslyn Art Museum, Omaha, Nebraska;
    Gift of Enron Art Foundation

23 Lap Desk, Parfleche
    Photography by Author

24 Sage Grouse
    Photography by J. Nevin Thompson

Beads
Photography by Terry McGrew, McGrew Photography
© Joyce Badgley Hunsaker and Towanda, Inc.

25 Seaman
    Seaside, OR. Photography by David B. Hunsaker

26 Arrowheads
    Photography by Terry McGrew, McGrew Photography
    © Joyce Badgley Hunsaker and Towanda, Inc.

27 Great Falls
    Photography by F. Jay Haynes, 1880
    Courtesy of the Haynes Foundation Collection,
    Montana Historical Society

    Canoe
    Original art by Gerald Arrington

    "Sailing Canoe"
    Montana State Parks, Missouri River

28 Bird
    Original art by Erica Thurston

29 Buffalo
    Original art by Erica Thurston

30 Beaverhead Mountains
    Photography by Jay W. Krajic

31 Feather
    Original art by Erica Thurston

32 Woman of the Snake Tribe, Vignette, Tableau 33
    Courtesy of the Joslyn Art Museum, Omaha, Nebraska;
    Gift of Enron Art Foundation

49　Weasel
Original art by Erica Thurston

Tobacco Twists
Photography by Terry McGrew, McGrew Photography
© Joyce Badgley Hunsaker and Towanda, Inc.

50　Saltworks
Courtesy of Fort Clatsop National Memorial-National
Park Service

51　Cedars, Mountain Bluebirds
Photography by Jay W. Krajic

52　Tiger Lily
Photography by Jay W. Krajic

Whale Bones
Original art by Erica Thurston

53　Gospel Hump
Photography by Jay W. Krajic

54　Castle Peak
Photography by Jay W. Krajic

55　Newfoundland Dog
Original art by Erica Thurston

Abalone
Photography by Terry McGrew, McGrew Photography
© Joyce Badgley Hunsaker and Towanda, Inc.

56　Buckskin Bag
Photography by Terry McGrew, McGrew Photography
© Joyce Badgley Hunsaker and Towanda, Inc.

57　Nez Perce Warrior's Possessions
Courtesy of USDA Forest Service, Lewis and Clark
National Historic Trail Interpretive Center, Great Falls

58　Pompey's Pillar
Photograph by L.A. Huffman, 1902
Courtesy of the Montana Historical Society, Helena,
Montana

59　Pictographs
Photography by Richard and Susan Donnelly

William Clark's Signature
USDI/BLM Pompey's Piller National Landmark,
Montana

60　Eagle, Spittle Bug
Photography by J. Nevin Thompson

Bear
Original art by Erica Thurston

61　Mandan Earth Lodge
Photograph by L.A. Huffman, 1902
Courtesy of the Montana Historical Society, Helena,
Montana

62　Turkey Feather Fan, Dentalium Necklace
Photography by Terry McGrew, McGrew Photography
© Joyce Badgley Hunsaker and Towanda, Inc.

63　Beargrass
Photography by Jay W. Krajic

64-65 Map
Corbis Images

Joyce Badgley Hunsaker

Joyce Badgley Hunsaker is an award-winning historical interpreter and story-teller. Her thoughtful and carefully researched programs have won her national acclaim as both performer and historian. For the past twenty years, she has performed her living histories around campfires, in schools and museums, on stage, and via national television and radio. She has opened legislative sessions, performed with symphonies, and developed historical vignettes with the NBA Portland Trailblazers. Ms. Hunsaker has given command performances in Washington, DC for such distinguished organizations as the Smithsonian Institution, the National Geographic Society, and ranking members of Congress. Her work is currently being used in Eastern Russia to teach American history and English.

Ms. Hunsaker's family lineage includes English, French, Cherokee, Scots-Irish, and Sioux. She has been honored by several tribes with ceremonial names. She has danced at Sun Dance, by invitation, and continues to walk the way of The Pipe.

Joyce Badgley Hunsaker and her husband David live in northeastern Oregon at the foot of the Elkhorn Mountains, within sight of Sacajawea Peak in the Land of the Winding Waters.